THE STORY OF SHAKESPEARE'S WORKS——ROMEO AND JULIET

莎士比亚名著故事——罗密欧与朱丽叶

[英] 查尔斯·兰姆 玛丽·兰姆 改编
蔡红昌 等编译

外文出版社
FOREIGN LANGUAGES PRESS

图书在版编目（CIP）数据

莎士比亚名著故事 . 罗密欧与朱丽叶 / 蔡红昌编译 . –
北京 : 外文出版社 , 2017
ISBN 978-7-119-10952-7

Ⅰ . ①莎… Ⅱ . ①蔡… Ⅲ . ①悲剧 – 剧本 – 英国 – 中世纪 Ⅳ . ① I561.33

中国版本图书馆 CIP 数据核字 (2017) 第 179822 号

出版策划 王京强
责任编辑 施化敏
责任校对 张志凡
封面设计 贺玉婷　魏芳芳
设计排版 北京维诺传媒文化有限公司
印刷监制 冯　浩

莎士比亚名著故事——罗密欧与朱丽叶
编　　译 蔡红昌　等

出版发行 外文出版社有限责任公司
地　　址 北京市西城区百万庄大街 24 号　　**邮政编码** 100037
网　　址 http://www.flp.com.cn
电　　话 010-68320579（总编室）010-68996179（编辑部）
印　　制 北京飞达印刷有限责任公司
经　　销 新华书店 / 外文书店
开　　本 710mm × 1000mm　1/16
印　　张 13.5　　　**字　　数** 257 千
版　　次 2017 年 8 月第 1 版第 1 次印刷
书　　号 ISBN 978-7-119-10952-7
定　　价 29.00 元

内容简介

本书收录了由英国著名作家玛丽·兰姆和查尔斯·兰姆姐弟改编的莎士比亚名著故事10篇。《罗密欧与朱丽叶》《麦克白》《李尔王》《哈姆雷特》《泰尔亲王伯利克里》和《辛白林》等世界公认的文学名篇，影响了一代又一代的人们。这些名著被翻译成世界上多种文字，并且被改编成戏剧、电影、电视剧、芭蕾舞、歌剧、木偶剧和卡通片等。无论作为语言学习的课本，还是作为了解莎士比亚作品的通俗读本，以简要、通俗的形式介绍这些经典名著故事对当代中国的青少年读者都将产生积极的影响。为了使读者能够了解英文故事概况，进而提高阅读速度和阅读水平，在每篇的开始部分增加了中文导读。同时，为了使读者更好地理解故事内容，书中加入了大量的插图。

前　言

威廉·莎士比亚（William Shakespeare，1564—1616），文艺复兴时期英国伟大的剧作家、诗人，被誉为“英国戏剧之父”“人类文学奥林匹斯山上的宙斯”。

1564 年 4 月 23 日，莎士比亚出生在英格兰沃里克郡斯特拉福镇一个比较富裕的家庭，父亲曾任该镇镇长。莎士比亚幼年在当地文法学校学习，并对戏剧、诗歌怀有浓厚的兴趣；13 岁时因家道衰败被迫辍学，18 岁结婚；约在 1586 年（或说 1587 年）前往伦敦谋生，先在剧院门前为贵族顾客看马，后逐渐成为剧院的杂役、演员、剧作家，最后成了剧院股东。

莎士比亚是英国文学史和戏剧史上最杰出的诗人和剧作家，也是西方文艺史上最杰出的作家之一、全世界最伟大的剧作家之一，是举世公认的文学天才。他一生共写有 37 部戏剧、154 首 14 行诗、两首长诗和其他诗歌等。莎士比亚的主要作品悲剧包括：《罗密欧与朱丽叶》《麦克白》《李尔王》《哈姆雷特》《奥赛罗》《泰特斯·安特洛尼克斯》《裘力斯·凯撒》《安东尼与克莉奥佩屈拉》《科利奥兰纳斯》《特洛埃围城记》《雅典的泰蒙》等，喜剧作品包括：《错误的喜剧》《终成眷属》《皆大欢喜》《仲夏夜之梦》《无事生非》《一报还一报》《暴风雨》《驯悍记》《第十二夜》《威尼斯商人》《温莎的风流娘们》《爱的徒劳》《维洛那二绅士》《提尔国王佩力克尔斯》《辛白林》《冬天的故事》等，历史剧：《亨利四世》《亨利五世》《亨利六世》《亨利八世》《约翰王》

《里查二世》《里查三世》，十四行诗包括：《爱人的怨诉》《鲁克丽丝失贞记》《维纳斯和阿多尼斯》《热情的朝圣者》《凤凰和斑鸠》等。

几个世纪以来，莎士比亚的作品一直影响着世界各地的读者，给世人留下了极其宝贵的精神财富，他的戏剧作品是世界文学史上的一座丰碑。他的作品被译成世界上几乎所有的文字，他的剧本至今还在世界各地演出。1616 年 4 月 26 日，莎士比亚在家乡的小镇去世，逝后被安葬在镇上的一个小教堂旁。每年来自世界各地数以千万计的人像朝圣一般去瞻仰他的墓地。在他生日的那天，每年都有许多国家的剧院在上演他的剧本纪念他。

在中国，莎士比亚是深受广大读者喜爱的作家，他们也是最早被介绍给中国读者的作家。为了让国内读者更好地了解莎士比亚作品，我们决定引进由英国著名作家玛丽·兰姆和查尔斯·兰姆姐弟改编的莎士比亚名著故事，并采用中文导读英文版的形式出版。在中文导读中，我们尽力使其贴近原作的精髓，也尽可能保留原作故事主线。我们希望能够编出为当代中国读者所喜爱的经典读本。读者在阅读英文故事之前，可以先阅读中文导读内容，这样有利于了解故事背景，从而加快阅读速度。我们相信，该经典著作的引进对提高当代中国读者，特别是青少年读者的人文修养是非常有帮助的。

本书由蔡红昌组织编译。参加本书编译工作的还有赵雪、刘乃亚、纪飞、陈起永、熊建国、程来川、龚武元、李毛华、徐平国、敖宗林、龚桂平、熊志勇、潘文华、陈凤英、谭学民、李丹妮、张灵羚、谭榜乾、付建平、汪疆玮、龚火荣、葛文聪、杨晓、葛文博、张雨、葛其昌、于丹等。限于我们的科学、人文素养和英语水平，书中难免会有不当之处，衷心希望读者朋友批评指正。

目　录

泰尔亲王伯利克里

Pericles, Prince of Tyre

导 读

由于泰尔亲王伯利克里发现了希腊皇帝暗中做的坏事，这个皇帝要报复泰尔城的百姓。为了避免灾难发生，伯利克里主动到海外流亡。泰尔则由能臣赫勒堪纽斯来管理。伯利克里首先到达了塔瑟斯，救济了这里的百姓，塔瑟斯总督克里翁和百姓都很感谢伯利克里。但是为了躲避希腊皇帝的追杀，伯利克里只好继续流亡。

不幸的伯利克里遇上了风暴，但他幸免于难，被渔夫救起。现在伯利克里正在本塔波利斯国，国王的女儿泰萨要在第二天生日的时候比武招亲。伯利克里很为自己丢失的铠甲惋惜，那是父亲的遗物，否则就可以穿着去比武了。这时渔夫把铠甲还给了伯利克里，原来铠甲也被渔夫打捞起来了。

伯利克里打败了所有的竞争者，一下子被本塔波利斯的国王看中，国王把自己的女儿泰萨嫁给了伯利克里，不过伯利克里为了躲避追杀并没有显露自己真正的身份。很快，伯利克里接到赫勒堪纽斯的消息，希腊皇帝死了，而泰尔城百姓要拥立赫勒堪纽斯，赫勒堪纽斯希望伯利克里尽快回来。

本塔波利斯的国王知道自己的女儿嫁给了亲王，很高兴，但是现在女儿怀着身孕，不得不跟伯利克里分别。不过泰萨坚持要与丈夫一起回国，国王和亲王都只好同意。

但是不幸的伯利克里在返回的途中又遇到了风暴，泰萨受了惊吓，生下孩子以后就不省人事了。伯利克里非常难过，但是为了祈求风暴平息，只好将死去的王后投入大海。伯利克里还在装有泰萨尸体的箱子上写明了泰萨的名字和身份，希望好心人能帮忙掩埋。这个箱子被塞利蒙捞起，塞利蒙不相信泰萨已经身亡，后来设法把泰萨救活，原来泰萨只是昏迷而已。

他被冲到海边的怪石上

泰萨看了丈夫的字条，以为丈夫在风暴中丧生，就去神庙里做了女祭司，虔诚祈祷。

而伯利克里这边，担心刚刚生下的女婴坚持不到泰尔，就在路过塔瑟斯的时候将其托付给了克里翁夫妇。克里翁夫妇答应会把这个女孩儿养大成人，并且接受最好的教育。伯利克里很放心，就把女儿玛莉娜的奶妈一起留了下来。

一晃十四年过去了，泰尔政通人和，玛莉娜也长大成人，而且多才多艺，深受大家喜爱，而克里翁自己的孩子则相差甚远，克里翁的妻子迪奥妮萨很是嫉妒。于是，这个女人决定趁玛莉娜为自己刚刚去世的奶妈哭泣的时候派人杀掉玛莉娜。迪奥妮萨先哄骗玛莉娜跟着仆人里欧奈恩去散步，然后让里欧奈恩趁机杀掉玛莉娜。

一路上玛莉娜都在讲着自己出生的那个故事，可里欧奈恩还是要杀掉玛莉娜，就在里欧奈恩将要动手的时候，玛莉娜被海盗掳走了。海盗把玛莉娜卖到了米迪林。由于玛莉娜很有才华，米迪林的总督赖斯莫克斯很尊重这个女孩儿，甚至想要弄清玛丽娜的底细，然后向玛莉娜求婚。

里欧奈恩回去撒谎说已经杀死了玛莉娜，迪奥妮萨就为玛莉娜立了一个墓碑。伯利克里来接自己的女儿，却只看到墓碑，他悲痛欲绝，在船上一声不吭，郁郁寡欢。伯利克里的船经过了米迪林，赖斯莫克斯前来迎接。赖斯莫克斯听说了亲王的状况，就把玛莉娜叫来，希望用玛莉娜的聪明才智使亲王恢复正常。

玛莉娜开始为亲王讲述自己的不幸，伯利克里觉得这个女孩儿很像自己死去的妻子，就问起了玛莉娜的身世。当亲王听说女孩就叫玛莉娜，还听说了女孩的其他经历，确信这是自己的女儿时，亲王欣喜若狂。这一晚，亲王做了一个奇怪的梦，梦里一个女神要亲王去艾菲索斯的神庙讲述自己的不幸，会让他遇到意外之喜。

第二天，赖斯莫克斯向玛莉娜求婚，亲王伯利克里要求自己的女儿和赖斯莫克斯先陪着自己去一趟艾菲索斯。亲王在艾菲索斯的神庙里诉说着自己的不幸，而这里的祭司正好就是泰萨，泰萨听出了亲王的声音，听了亲王的经历之后，泰萨喊着亲王的名字晕倒了。这时塞利蒙告诉亲王这个祭司就是泰萨，又把泰萨当年的经历告诉亲王。亲王非常高兴，现在一家人终于团聚了，而泰萨也同意赖斯莫克斯迎娶自己的女儿玛莉娜。

品行端正的人历经千辛万苦终得圆满，而对像迪奥妮萨这样的坏人，塔瑟斯的百姓非常生气，火烧王宫，克里翁和迪奥妮萨都被烧死了。

人物事件词汇表

Tyre	泰尔 古菲尼基的港口，现在黎巴嫩
Pericles	伯利克里 泰尔的统治者，一位英明的亲王
Helicanus	赫勒堪纽斯 泰尔亲王的能臣，一位正直的大臣
Thrsus	塔瑟斯 古国西里西亚的首府
Cleon	克里翁 塔瑟斯的总督
Pentapolis	本塔波利斯 希腊文，意为“五座城”，疑为古希腊在北非利比亚的殖民地
Thaisa	泰萨 伯利克里的王后，本塔波利斯国王的女儿
Cerimon	塞利蒙 艾菲索斯一个有名望的人，略懂医术
Dionysia	迪奥妮萨 克里翁的妻子，一个妒贤嫉能的女人
Marina	玛莉娜 伯利克里的女儿，名字的意思是“海女”，在海上而生
Leonine	里欧奈恩 迪奥妮萨的仆人
Mitylene	米迪林 希腊的一个岛屿，在爱琴海中
Lysimachus	赖斯莫克斯 米迪林的总督，娶了伯利克里的女儿玛莉娜

Pericles, prince of Tyre, became a voluntary exile from his dominions, to avert the dreadful calamities which Antiochus, the wicked emperor of Greece, threatened to bring upon his subjects and city of Tyre, in revenge for a discovery which the prince had made of a shocking deed which the emperor had done in secret; as commonly it proves dangerous to pry into the hidden crimes of great ones. Leaving the government of his people in the hands of his able and honest minister, Helicanus, Pericles set sail from Tyre, thinking to absent himself till the wrath of Antiochus, who was mighty, should be appeased.

The first place which the prince directed his course to was Tarsus, and hearing that the city of Tarsus was at that time suffering under a severe famine, he took with him store of provisions for its relief. On his arrival he found the city reduced to the utmost distress; and, he coming like a messenger from heaven with his unhoped-for succour, Cleon, the governor of Tarsus, welcomed him with boundless thanks. Pericles had not been here many days, before letters came from his faithful minister, warning him that it was not safe for him to stay at Tarsus, for Antiochus knew of his abode, and by secret emissaries despatched for that purpose sought his life. Upon receipt of these letters Pericles put out to sea again, amidst the blessings and prayers of a whole people who had been fed by his bounty.

He had not sailed far, when his ship was overtaken by a dreadful storm, and every man on board perished except Pericles, who was cast by the sea-waves naked on an unknown shore, where he had not wandered long before he met with some poor fishermen, who invited him to their homes, giving him clothes and provisions. The fishermen told Pericles the name of their country was Pentapolis, and that their king was Simonides, commonly called the good Simonides, because of his peaceable reign and good government. From them he also learned that king Simonides had a fair young daughter, and that the following day was her birthday, when a grand tournament was to be held at court, many princes and knights being come from all parts to try their skill in arms for the love of Thaisa, this fair princess. While the prince was listening to this account, and secretly lamenting the loss of his good armour, which disabled him from making one among these valiant knights, another fisherman brought in a complete suit of armour that he had taken out of the sea with his fishing-net, which proved to be the very armour he had lost. When Pericles beheld his own armour, he said: 'Thanks, Fortune; after all my crosses you give me somewhat to repair myself. This armour was bequeathed to me by my dead father, for whose dear sake I have so loved it that whithersoever I went, I still have kept it by me, and the rough sea that parted it from me, having now become calm, hath given it back again, for which I thank it for, since I have my father's gift again, I think my shipwreck no misfortune.'

The next day Pericles clad in his brave father's armour, repaired to the royal court of Simonides, where he performed wonders at the tournament, vanquishing with ease all the brave knights and valiant princes who contended with him in arms for the honour of Thaisa's love. When brave warriors contended at court tournaments for the love of king's daughters, if one proved sole victor over all the rest, it was usual for the great lady for whose sake these deeds of velour were undertaken, to bestow all her respect upon the conqueror, and Thaisa did not depart from this custom, for she presently dismissed all the princes and knights whom Pericles had vanquished, and distinguished him by her especial favour and regard, crowning him with the

穿上了盔甲

wrath of victory, as king of that day's happiness; and Pericles became a most passionate lover of this beauteous princess from the first moment he beheld her.

The good Simonides so well approved of the velour and noble qualities of Pericles, who was indeed a most accomplished gentleman, and well learned in all excellent arts, that though he knew not the rank of this royal stranger (for Pericles for fear of Antiochus gave out that he was a private gentleman of Tyre), yet did not Simonides disdain to accept of the valiant unknown for a son-in-law, when he perceived his daughter's affections were firmly fixed upon him.

Pericles had not been many months married to Thaisa, before he received intelligence that his enemy Antiochus was dead, and that his subjects of Tyre, impatient of his long absence, threatened to revolt, and talked of placing Helicanus upon his vacant throne. This news came from Helicanus himself, who, being a loyal subject to his royal master, would not accept of the high dignity offered him, but sent to let Pericles know their intentions, that he might return home and resume his lawful right. It was matter of great surprise and joy to Simonides, to find that his son-in-law (the obscure knight) was the renowned prince of Tyre; yet again he regretted that he was not the private gentleman he supposed him to be, seeing that he must now part both with his admired son-in-law and his beloved daughter, whom he feared to trust to the perils of the sea, because Thaisa was with child; and Pericles himself wished her

泰萨请求一起回国

to remain with her father till after her confinement, but the poor lady so earnestly desired to go with her husband, that at last they consented, hoping she would reach Tyre before she was brought to bed.

The sea was no friendly element to unhappy Pericles, for long before they reached Tyre another dreadful tempest arose, which so terrified Thaisa that she was taken ill, and in a short space of time her nurse Lychorida came to Pericles with a little child in her arms, to tell the prince the sad tidings that his wife died the moment her little babe was born. She held the babe towards its father, saying: 'Here is a thing too young for such a place. This is the child of your dead queen.' No tongue can tell the dreadful sufferings of Pericles when he heard his wife was dead. As soon as he could speak, he said: 'O you gods, why do you make us love your goodly gifts, and then snatch those gifts away?' 'Patience,

王后被人救起

good sir,' said Lychorida, 'here is all that is left alive of our dead queen, a little daughter, and for your child's sake be more manly. Patience, good sir, even for the sake of this precious charge.' Pericles took the new-born infant in his arms, and he said to the little babe: 'Now may your life be mild, for a more blusterous birth had never babe! May your condition be mild and gentle, for you have had the rudest welcome that ever prince's child did meet with! May that which follows be happy, for you have had as chiding a nativity as fire, air, water, earth, and heaven could make to herald you from the womb! Even at the first, your loss,' meaning in the death of her mother, 'is more than all the joys, which you shall find upon this earth to which you are come a new visitor, shall be able to recompense.'

The storm still continuing to rage furiously, and the sailors having a superstition that while a dead body remained in the ship the storm would never cease, they came to Pericles to demand that his queen should be thrown overboard; and they said: 'What courage, sir? God save you!' 'Courage enough,' said the sorrowing prince: 'I do not fear the storm; it has done to me its worst; yet for the love of this poor infant, this fresh new seafarer, I wish the storm was over.' 'Sir,' said the sailors, 'your queen must overboard. The sea works high, the wind is loud, and the storm will not abate till the ship be cleared of the dead.' Though Pericles knew how weak and unfounded this superstition was, yet he patiently submitted, saying: 'As you think meet. Then she must overboard, most wretched queen!' And now this unhappy prince went to take a last view of his dear wife, and as he looked on his Thaisa, he said: 'A terrible childbed hast thou had, my dear; no light, no fire; the unfriendly elements forget thee utterly, nor have I time to bring thee hallowed to thy grave, but must cast thee scarcely coffined into the sea, where for a monument upon thy bones the humming waters must overwhelm thy corpse, lying with simple shells. O Lychorida, bid Nestor bring me spices, ink, and paper, my casket and my jewels, and bid Nicandor bring me the satin coffin. Lay the babe upon the pillow, and go about this suddenly, Lychorida, while I say a priestly farewell to my Thaisa.'

王后被放进箱子

They brought Pericles a large chest, in which (wrapped in a satin shroud) he placed his queen, and sweet-smelling spices he strewed over her, and beside her he placed rich jewels, and a written paper, telling who she was, and praying if haply any one should find the chest which contained the body of his wife, they would give her burial: and then with his own hands he cast the chest into the sea. When the storm was over, Pericles ordered the sailors to make for Tarsus. 'For,' said Pericles, 'the babe cannot hold out till we come to Tyre. At Tarsus I will leave it at careful nursing.'

After that tempestuous night when Thaisa was thrown into the sea, and while it was yet early morning, as Cerimon, a worthy gentleman of Ephesus, and a most skilful physician, was standing by the sea-side, his servants brought to him a chest, which they said the sea-waves had thrown on the land. 'I never saw,' said one of them, 'so huge a billow as cast it on our shore.' Cerimon ordered the chest to be conveyed to his own house and when it was opened he beheld with wonder the body of a young and lovely lady; and the sweet-smelling spices and rich casket of jewels made him conclude it was some great person who was thus strangely entombed: searching farther, he discovered a paper, from which he learned that the corpse which lay as dead before him had been a queen, and wife to Pericles, prince of Tyre; and much admiring at the strangeness of that accident, and more pitying the husband who had lost this sweet lady, he said: 'If you are living, Pericles, you have a heart that even cracks with woe.' Then observing attentively Thaisa's face, he saw how fresh and unlike death her looks were, and he said: 'They were too hasty that threw you into the sea': for he did not believe her to be dead. He ordered a fire to be made, and proper cordials to be brought, and soft music to be played, which might help to calm her amazed spirits if she should revive; and he said to those who crowded round her, wondering at what they saw: 'I pray you, gentlemen, give her air; this queen will live; she has not been entranced above five hours; and see, she begins to blow into life again; she is alive; behold, her eyelids move; this fair creature will live to make us weep to hear her fate.' Thaisa had never died, but after the birth of her little baby had fallen into a deep swoon, which made all that saw her conclude her to be dead; and now by the care of this kind gentleman she once more revived to light and life; and opening her eyes, she said: 'Where am I? Where is my lord? What world is this?' By gentle degrees Cerimon let her understand what had befallen her; and when he thought she was enough recovered to bear the sight, he showed her the paper written by her husband, and the jewels; and she looked on the paper, and said: 'It is my lord's writing. That I was shipped at sea, I well remember, but whether there delivered of my babe, by the holy gods I cannot rightly say; but since my wedded lord I never shall see again, I will put on a vestal livery, and never more have joy.' 'Madam,' said Cerimon, 'if you purpose as you speak, the temple of Diana is not far distant from hence; there you may abide as a vestal. Moreover, if you please, a niece of mine shall there attend you.' This proposal was accepted with thanks by Thaisa; and when she was perfectly recovered, Cerimon placed her in the temple of Diana, where she became a vestal or priestess of that goddess, and passed her days in sorrowing for her husband's supposed loss, and in the most devout exercises of those times.

Pericles carried his young daughter (whom he named Marina, because she was born at sea) to Tarsus, intending to leave her with Cleon, the governor of that city, and his wife Dionysia, thinking, for the good he had done to them at the time of their famine, they would be kind to his little motherless daughter. When Cleon saw prince Pericles, and heard of the great loss which had befallen him, he said: 'O your sweet queen, that it had pleased Heaven you could have brought her hither to have blessed my eyes with the sight of her!' Pericles replied: 'We must obey the powers above us. Should I rage and roar as the sea does in which my Thaisa lies, yet the end must be as it is. My gentle babe, Marina here, I must charge your charity with her. I leave her the infant of your care, beseeching you to give her princely training.' And then turning to Cleon's wife, Dionysia, he said: 'Good madam, make me blessed in your care in bringing up my child': and she answered: 'I have a child myself who shall not be more dear to my respect than yours, my lord'; and Cleon made the like promise, saying: 'Your noble services, prince Pericles, in feeding my whole people with your corn (for which in their prayers they daily remember you) must in your child be thought on. If I should neglect your child, my whole people that were by you relieved would force me to my duty; but if to that I need a spur, the gods revenge it on me and mine to the end of generation.' Pericles being thus assured that his child would be carefully attended to, left her to the protection of Cleon and his wife Dionysia, and with her he left the nurse Lychorida. When he went away, the little Marina knew not her loss, but Lychorida wept sadly at parting with her royal master. 'O, no tears, Lychorida,' said Pericles: 'no tears; look to your little mistress, on whose grace you may depend hereafter.'

Pericles arrived in safety at Tyre, and was once more settled in the quiet possession of his throne, while his woeful queen, whom he thought dead, remained at Ephesus. Her little babe Marina, whom this hapless mother had never seen, was brought up by Cleon in a manner suitable to her high birth. He gave her the most careful education, so that by the time Marina attained the age of fourteen years, the most deeply-learned men were not more studied in the learning of those times than was Marina. She sang like one immortal, and danced as goddesslike, and with her needle she was so skilful that she seemed to compose nature's own shapes, in birds, fruits, or flowers, the natural roses being scarcely more like to each other than they were to Marina's silken flowers. But when she had gained from education all these graces, which made her the general wonder, Dionysia, the wife of Cleon, became her mortal enemy from jealousy, by reason that her own daughter, from the slowness of her mind, was not able to attain to that perfection wherein Marina excelled: and finding that all praise was bestowed on Marina, whilst her daughter, who was of the same age, and had been educated with the same care as Marina, though not with the same success, was in comparison disregarded, she formed a project to remove Marina out of the way, vainly imagining that her untoward daughter would be more respected when Marina was no more seen. To encompass this she employed a man to murder Marina, and she well timed her wicked design, when Lychorida, the faithful nurse, had just died. Dionysia was discoursing with the man she had commanded to

美丽的玛丽娜

commit this murder, when the young Marina was weeping over the dead Lychorida. Leonine, the man she employed to do this bad deed, though he was a very wicked man, could hardly be persuaded to undertake it, so had Marina won all hearts to love her. He said: 'She is a goodly creature!' 'The tatter then the gods should have her,' replied her merciless enemy: 'here she comes weeping for the death of her nurse Lychorida: are you resolved to obey me?' Leonine, fearing to disobey her, replied: 'I am resolved.' And so, in that one short sentence, was the matchless Marina doomed to an untimely death. She now approached, with a basket of flowers in her hand, which she said she would daily strew over the grave of good Lychorida. The purple violet and the marigold should as a carpet hang upon her grave, while summer days did last. 'Alas, for me!' she said, 'poor unhappy maid, born in a tempest, when my mother died. This world to me is like a lasting storm, hurrying me from my friends.' 'How now, Marina,' said the dissembling Dionysia, 'do you weep alone? How does it chance my daughter is not with you? Do not sorrow for Lychorida, you have a nurse in me. Your beauty is quite changed with this unprofitable woe. Come, give me your flowers, the sea-air will spoil them; and walk with Leonine: the air is fine, and will enliven you. Come, Leonine, take her by the arm, and walk with her.' 'No, madam,' said Marina, 'I pray you let me not deprive you of your servant': for Leonine was one of Dionysia's attendants. 'Come, come,' said this artful woman, who wished for a presence to leave her alone with Leonine, 'I love the prince, your father, and I love you. We every day expect your father here; and when he comes, and finds you so changed by grief from the paragon of beauty we reported you, he will think we have taken no care of you. Go, I pray you, walk, and be cheerful once again. Be careful of that excellent complexion, which stole the hearts of old and young.' Marina, being thus importuned, said: 'Well, I will go, but yet I have no desire to it.' As Dionysia walked away, she said to Leonine: 'Remember what I have said!'—shocking words, for their meaning was that he should remember to kill Marina.

Marina looked towards the sea, her birthplace, and said: 'Is the wind westerly that blows?' 'South-west,' replied Leonine. 'When I was born the wind was north,' said she: and then the storm and tempest, and all her father's sorrows, and her mother's death, came full into her mind; and she said: 'My father, as Lychorida told me, did never fear, but cried, Courage, good seamen, to the sailors, galling his princely hands with the ropes, and, clasping to the masts, he endured a sea that almost split the deck.' 'When was this?' said Leonine. 'When I was born,' replied Marina: 'never were wind and waves more violent'; and then she described the storm, the action of the sailors, the boatswain's whistle, and the loud call of the master, 'which,' said she, 'trebled the confusion of the ship.' Lychorida had so often recounted to Marina the story of her hapless birth that these things seemed ever present to her imagination. But here Leonine interrupted her with desiring her to say her prayers. 'What mean you?' said Marina, who began to fear, she knew not why. 'If you require a little space for prayer, I grant it,' said Leonine; 'but be not tedious, the gods are quick of ear, and I am sworn to do my work in haste.' 'Will you kill me?' said Marina: 'alas! why?' 'To satisfy my lady,' replied Leonine. 'Why would she have me killed?' said Marina: 'now, as I can remember, I never hurt her in all my life. I never spake bad word, nor did any ill turn to any living creature. Believe me now, I never killed a mouse, nor hurt a fly. I trod upon a worm once against my will, but I wept for it. How have I offended?' The murderer replied: 'My commission is not to reason on the deed, but to do it.' And he was just going to kill her, when certain pirates happened to land at that very moment, who seeing Marina, bore her off as a prize to their ship.

The pirate who had made Marina his prize carried her to Mitylene, and sold her for a slave, where, though in that humble condition, Marina soon became known throughout the whole city of Mitylene for her beauty and her virtues; and the person to whom she was sold became rich by the money she earned for him. She taught music, dancing, and fine needleworks, and the money she got by her scholars she gave to her master and mistress; and the fame of her learning and her great industry came to the knowledge of Lysimachus, a young nobleman who was governor of Mitylene, and Lysimachus went himself to the house where Marina dwelt, to see this paragon of excellence, whom all the city praised so highly. Her conversation delighted Lysimachus beyond measure, for though he had heard much of this admired maiden, he did not expect to find her so sensible a lady, so virtuous, and so good, as he perceived Marina to be; and he left her, saying, he hoped she would persevere in her industrious and virtuous course, and that if ever she heard from him again it should be for her good. Lysimachus thought Marina such a miracle for sense, fine breeding, and excellent qualities, as well as for beauty and all outward graces, that he wished to marry her, and notwithstanding her humble situation, he hoped to find that her birth was noble; but ever when they asked her parentage she would sit still and weep.

Meantime, at Tarsus, Leonine, fearing the anger of Dionysia, told her he had killed Marina; and that wicked woman gave out that she was dead, and made a pretended funeral for her, and erected a stately monument; and shortly after Pericles, accompanied by his royal minister Helicanus, made a voyage from Tyre to Tarsus, on purpose to see his daughter, intending to take her home with him: and he never having beheld her since he left her an infant in the care of Cleon and his wife, how did this good prince rejoice at the thought of seeing this dear child of his buried queen! but when they told him Marina was dead, and showed the monument they had erected for her, great was the misery this most wretched father endured, and not being able to bear the sight of that country where his last hope and only memory of his dear Thaisa was entombed, he took ship, and hastily departed from Tarsus. From the day he entered the ship a dull and heavy melancholy seized him. He never spoke, and seemed totally insensible to everything around him.

Sailing from Tarsus to Tyre, the ship in its course passed by Mitylene, where Marina dwelt; the governor of which place, Lysimachus, observing this royal vessel from the shore, and desirous of knowing who was on board, went in a barge to the side of the ship, to satisfy his curiosity. Helicanus received him very courteously and told him that the ship came from Tyre, and that they were conducting thither Pericles, their prince; 'A man, sir,' said Helicanus, 'who has not spoken to any one these three months, nor taken any sustenance, but just to prolong his grief; it would be tedious to repeat the whole ground of his distemper, but the main springs from the loss of a beloved daughter and a wife.' Lysimachus begged to see this afflicted prince, and when he beheld Pericles, he saw he had been once a goodly person, and he said to him: 'Sir king, all hail, the gods preserve you, hail, royal sir!' But in vain Lysimachus spoke to him; Pericles made no answer, nor did he appear to perceive any stranger approached. And then Lysimachus bethought him of the peerless maid Marina, that haply with her sweet tongue she might win some answer from the silent prince: and with the consent of Helicanus he sent for Marina, and when she entered the ship in which her own father sat motionless with grief, they welcomed her on board as if they had known she was their princess; and they cried: 'She is a gallant lady.' Lysimachus was well pleased to hear their commendations, and he said: 'She is such a one, that were I well assured she came of noble birth, I would wish no better choice, and think me rarely blessed in a wife.' And then he addressed her in courtly terms, as if the lowly-seeming maid had been the high-born lady he wished to find her, calling her Fair and beautiful Marina, telling her a great prince on board that ship had fallen into a sad and mournful silence; and, as if Marina had the power of conferring health and felicity, he begged she would undertake to cure the royal stranger of his melancholy. 'Sir,' said Marina, 'I will use my utmost skill in his recovery, provided none but I and my maid be suffered to come near him.'

She, who at Mitylene had so carefully concealed her birth, ashamed to tell that one of royal ancestry was now a slave, first began to speak to Pericles of the wayward changes in her own fate, telling him from what a high estate herself had fallen. As if she had known it was her royal father she stood before, all the words she spoke were of her own sorrows; but her reason for so doing was, that she knew nothing more wins the attention of the unfortunate

对着父亲唱起了歌

than the recital of some sad calamity to match their own. The sound of her sweet voice aroused the drooping prince; he lifted up his eyes, which had been so long fixed and motionless; and Marina, who was the perfect image of her mother, presented to his amazed sight the features of his dead queen. The long-silent prince was once more heard to speak. 'My dearest wife,' said the awakened Pericles, 'was like this maid, and such a one might my daughter have been. My queen's square brows, her stature to an inch, as wand-like straight, as silver-voiced, her eyes as jewel-like. Where do you live, young maid? Report your parentage. I think you said you had been tossed from wrong to injury, and that you thought your griefs would equal mine, if both were opened.' 'Some such thing I said,' replied Marina, 'and said no more than what my thoughts did warrant me as likely.' 'Tell me your story,' answered Pericles; 'if I find you have known the thousandth part of my endurance, you have borne your sorrows like a man, and I have suffered like a girl; yet you do look like Patience gazing on kings' graves, and smiling extremity out of act. How lost you your name, my most kind virgin? Recount your story I beseech you. Come, sit by me.' How was Pericles surprised when she said her name was Marina, for he knew it was no usual name, but had been invented by himself for his own child to signify seaborn: 'O, I am mocked,' said he, 'and you are sent hither by some incensed god to make the world laugh at me.' 'Patience, good sir,' said Marina, 'or I must cease here.' 'Nay,' said Pericles, 'I will be patient; you little know how you do startle me, to call yourself Marina.' 'The name,' she replied, 'was given me by one that had some power, my father, and a king.' 'How, a king's daughter!' said Pericles, 'and called Marina! But are you flesh and blood? Are you no fairy? Speak on; where were you born? and wherefore called Marina?' She replied: 'I was called Marina, because I was born at sea. My mother was the daughter of a king; she died the minute I was born, as my good nurse Lychorida has often told me weeping. The king, my father, left me at Tarsus, till the cruel wife of Cleon sought to murder me. A crew of pirates came and rescued me, and brought me here to Mitylene. But, good sir, why do you weep? It may be, you think me an impostor. But, indeed, sir, I am the daughter to king Pericles, if good king Pericles be living.' Then Pericles, terrified as he seemed at his own sudden joy, and doubtful if this could be real, loudly called for his attendants, who rejoiced at the sound of their beloved king's voice; and he said to Helicanus: 'O Helicanus, strike me, give me a gash, put me to present pain, lest this great sea of joys rushing upon me, overbear the shores of my mortality. O, come hither, thou that west born at sea, buried at Tarsus, and found at sea again. O Helicanus, down on your knees, thank the holy gods! This is Marina. Now blessings on thee, my child! Give me fresh garments, mine own Helicanus! She is not dead at Tarsus as she should have been by the savage Dionysia. She shall tell you all, when you shall kneel to her and call her your very princess. Who is this?' (observing Lysimachus for the first time). 'Sir,' said Helicanus, 'it is the governor of Mitylene, who, hearing of your melancholy, came to see you.' 'I embrace you, sir,' said Pericles. 'Give me my robes! I am wild with beholding—O heaven bless my girl! But hark, what music is that?'—for now, either sent by some kind god, or by his own delighted fancy deceived, he seemed to hear soft music. 'My lord, I hear none,' replied Helicanus. 'None?' said Pericles; 'why it is the music of the spheres.' As there was no music to be heard, Lysimachus concluded that the sudden joy had unsettled the prince's understanding; and he said: 'It is not good to cross him: let him have his way': and then they told him they heard the music; and he now complaining of a drowsy slumber coming over him, Lysimachus persuaded him to rest on a couch, and placing a pillow under his head, he, quite overpowered with excess of joy, sank into a sound sleep, and Marina watched in silence by the couch of her sleeping parent.

While he slept, Pericles dreamed a dream which made him resolve to go to Ephesus. His dream was, that Diana, the goddess of the Ephesians, appeared to him, and commanded him to go to her temple at Ephesus, and there before her altar to declare the story of his life and misfortunes; and by her silver bow she swore, that if he performed her injunction, he should meet with some rate felicity. When he awoke, being miraculously refreshed, he told his dream, and that his resolution was to obey the bidding of the goddess.

Then Lysimachus invited Pericles to come on shore, and refresh himself with such entertainment as he should find at Mitylene, which courteous offer Pericles accepting, agreed to tarry with him for the space of a day or two. During which time we may well suppose what feastings, what rejoicings, what costly shows and entertainments the governor made in Mitylene, to greet the royal father of his dear Marina, whom in her obscure fortunes he had so respect-

来到神庙

ed. Nor did Pericles frown upon Lysimachus's suit, when he understood how he had honoured his child in the days of her low estate, and that Marina showed herself not averse to his proposals; only he made it a condition, before he gave his consent, that they should visit with him the shrine of the Ephesian Diana: to whose temple they shortly after all three undertook a voyage; and, the goddess herself filling their sails with prosperous winds, after a few weeks they arrived in safety at Ephesus.

There was standing near the altar of the goddess, when Pericles with his train entered the temple, the good Cerimon (now grown very aged) who had restored Thaisa, the wife of Pericles, to life; and Thaisa, now a priestess of the temple, was standing before the altar; and though the many years he had passed in sorrow for her loss had much altered Pericles, Thaisa thought she knew her husband's features, and when he approached the altar and began to speak, she remembered his voice, and listened to his words with wonder and a joyful amazement. And these were the words that Pericles spoke before the altar: 'Hail, Diana! to perform thy just commands, I here confess myself the prince of Tyre, who, frighted from my country, at Pentapolis wedded the fair Thaisa: she died at sea in childbed, but brought forth a maid-child called Marina. She at Tarsus was nursed with Dionysia, who at fourteen years thought to kill her, but her better stars brought her to Mitylene, by whose shores as I sailed, her good fortunes brought this maid on board, where by her most clear remembrance she made herself known to be my daughter.'

Thaisa, unable to bear the transports which his words had raised in her, cried out: 'You are, you are, O royal Pericles'—and fainted. 'What means this woman?' said Pericles: 'she dies! gentlemen, help.' 'Sir,' said Cerimon, 'if you have told Diana's altar true, this is your wife.' 'Reverend gentleman, no,' said Pericles: 'I threw her overboard with these very arms.' Cerimon then recounted how, early one tempestuous morning, this lady was thrown upon the Ephesian shore; how, opening the coffin, he found therein rich jewels, and a paper; how, happily, he recovered her, and placed her here in Diana's temple. And now,

Thaisa being restored from her swoon said: 'O my lord, are you not Pericles? Like him you speak, like him you are. Did you not name a tempest, a birth, and death?' He astonished said: 'The voice of dead Thaisa!' 'That Thaisa am I,' she replied, 'supposed dead and drowned.' 'O true Diana!' exclaimed Pericles, in a passion of devout astonishment. 'And now,' said Thaisa, 'I know you better. Such a ring as I see on your finger did the king my father give you, when we with tears parted from him at Pentapolis.' 'Enough, you gods!' cried Pericles, 'your present kindness makes my past miseries sport. O come, Thaisa, be buried a second time within these arms.

And Marina said: 'My heart leaps to be gone into my mother's bosom.' Then did Pericles show his daughter to her mother, saying: 'Look who kneels here, flesh of thy flesh, thy burthen at sea, and called Marina, because she was yielded there.' 'Blessed and my own!' said Thaisa: and while she hung in rapturous joy over her child, Pericles knelt before the altar, saying: 'Pure Diana, bless thee for thy vision. For this, I will offer oblations nightly to thee.' And then and there did Pericles, with the consent of Thaisa, solemnly affiance their daughter, the virtuous Marina, to the well-deserving Lysimachus in marriage.

Thus have we seen in Pericles, his queen, and daughter, a famous example of virtue assailed by calamity (through the sufferance of Heaven, to teach patience and constancy to men), under the same guidance becoming finally successful, and triumphing over chance and change. In Helicanus we have beheld a notable pattern of truth, of faith, and loyalty, who, when he might have succeeded to a shone, chose rather to recall the rightful owner to his possession, than to become great by another's wrong. In the worthy Cerimon, who restored Thaisa to life, we are instructed how goodness directed by knowledge, in bestowing benefits upon mankind, approaches to the nature of the gods. It only remains to be told, that Dionysia, the wicked wife of Cleon, met with an end proportionable to her deserts; the inhabitants of Tarsus, when her cruel attempt upon Marina was known, rising in a body to revenge the daughter of their benefactor, and setting fire to the palace of Cleon, burnt both him and her, and their whole household: the gods seeming well pleased, that so foul a murder, though but intentional, and never carried into act, should be punished in a way befitting its enormity.

李尔王
King Lear

导　读

不列颠国王李尔有三个女儿。法兰西国王和勃艮第公爵同时向李尔王的小女儿科迪莉亚求婚，这时都住在李尔的宫里。

李尔八十多岁了，身体已经衰弱，他决定让年轻人来治理国家。他把三个女儿叫到身边，想要听听三个女儿对自己的爱有多少，并且根据爱的多少来分配国土给她们。

大女儿贡纳莉用甜言蜜语哄骗李尔，其实她的心里一点儿也不爱自己的父亲。李尔被大女儿的花言巧语所蒙骗，把三分之一的国土分给了大女儿。

二女儿里根和姐姐一样，并不爱自己的父亲，但她也虚伪地对父亲诉说自己爱他。李尔也相信了二女儿的话，也把三分之一的国土分给了她。

轮到李尔最疼爱的小女儿向他诉说了。小女儿科迪莉亚刚才听着两位姐姐虚伪的话语，内心十分厌恶。她知道两位姐姐只是希望骗得国土，内心里并不爱自己的父亲。而她确确实实内心充满了对父亲的爱，但这份爱更多的是无声无息。所以她告诉李尔，她的爱不多不少，照着女儿的本分去爱着父亲。李尔不喜欢小女儿说的话，有些生气了。科迪莉亚还对李尔说，如果自己真的全心全意地爱着父亲，那就没有办法去爱自己的丈夫，那未来就不会像姐姐一样结婚了。

科迪莉亚

这些话激怒了老国王，他觉得自己的小女儿不爱自己，性格暴躁的他决定把原本应该分给小女儿的国土平分给了大女儿和二女儿，并且当众交出了国王的权力。他只提出了一个条件：未来他要在两个女儿的王宫里每个月轮流居住。

李尔王的朝臣肯特觉得老国王的决定太荒唐了，他劝说国王，希望国王能收回命令。他替科迪莉亚说好话，他用性命担保科迪莉亚对国王的爱绝对不比她的姐姐们差。但是这时候的李尔王根本听不进肯特的劝说。他驱逐了肯特，要求肯特立刻离开不列颠的土地。于是肯特离开了。

因为科迪莉亚无法继承父亲的国土，勃艮第公爵立刻决定不再向她求婚。但法兰西国王仍然坚持自己对科迪莉亚的爱，他了解科迪莉亚之所以失去父亲的宠爱只是因为她不擅长花言巧语，她的品德是她最可贵的嫁妆。于是，科迪莉亚远嫁去了法兰西。临别时，两位姐姐不停地嘲讽妹妹。科迪莉亚不放心自己的父亲，但是又没有办法，只能离开了。

科迪莉亚刚走，她的姐姐们就卸下了伪装。按照约定，李尔的第一个月住在大女儿贡纳莉的宫里。贡纳莉得到了她想要得到的一切，于是她开始讨厌自己的父亲，她找出各种理由躲着父亲，正是由于她的态度，连仆人对待李尔的态度都越来越冷淡。李尔装作看不出这种变化，因为他无法接受自己固执所犯下的错误。

那位被驱逐的肯特，对老国王一直忠心耿耿。他化妆成一个粗鲁的仆人，要求国王雇佣他。李尔没有看出这就是当年位高权重的肯特，只以为自己雇佣了一个普通的仆人凯厄斯。凯厄斯替李尔教训了贡纳莉的傲慢管家，这让他和李尔的关系越来越亲近了。

同时跟在李尔身边的还有一位正直的大臣，他编了很多曲子讽刺李尔错误的决定，让他现在沦入这么凄惨的地步，连下人都敢欺负他。

贡纳莉不仅仅对父亲越来越冷淡，同时她要求李尔去掉自己的排场，削减侍从的数量，这让李尔受不了了。他大声咒骂大女儿，用最恶毒的语言攻击她。贡纳莉的丈夫奥尔巴尼公爵向老国王解释说这一切自己并没有参与，但李尔根本听不进去。他决定到二女儿里根那里去。这时候李尔才感到自己对待小女儿科迪莉亚太过分了。

李尔派凯厄斯去给二女儿送信，恰巧碰到了同样给里根送信的贡纳莉的信使。这个信使就是当初被凯厄斯教训过的管家。凯厄斯再次狠狠地教训了那个管家。里根听说了这件事，就给凯厄斯戴上了脚枷。这样李尔走进城堡首先看到的就是自己忠心的仆人屈辱地坐在那里。

李尔要求二女儿来见自己，却被拒绝了。在他的一再坚持下，二女儿同他见了面，同时大女儿贡纳莉也一起来了。里根劝李尔回到姐姐那里，并且听从姐姐的安排。李尔觉得自己需要到女儿那里讨吃讨穿太荒唐了，坚持要在二女儿这里住。于是里根也提出了自己的要求，她也要求李尔减少仆从。两个女儿像是在比赛一样剥夺着李尔曾经作为国王的尊严，而且越来越过分。李尔一方面受到虐待，一方面后悔自己抛弃了国家，他的神志开始不正常了。

外面狂风暴雨，李尔和他的侍从被女儿从家中驱逐出去。在大雨中，李尔越发不清醒了，他感觉自己实在是最糊涂的人，他的内心充满了对两个忘恩负义的女儿的恨。凯厄斯把李尔安顿在了一个仍忠于国王的城堡里，自己兼程赶到了科迪莉亚的王宫。听到父亲的悲惨境遇，科迪莉亚要求她的丈夫允许自己带领人马去讨伐那两个恶毒的女人。于是她带领自己的军队回到了不列颠。

科迪莉亚见到了有些精神失常的李尔，她派了最高明的医生医治李尔。这时候的李尔神志越发不清醒，他已经认不出科迪莉亚了。但是他仍希望能够得到女儿的原谅，对于自己过去因为固执所犯下的错，他感到深深的悔恨。科迪莉亚安慰着李尔，她发誓自己会永远爱自己的父亲，会好好地照顾他。

大女儿贡纳莉和二女儿里根现在更加肆无忌惮。她们对待自己的丈夫也不再忠诚。她们同时喜欢上了一个叫做埃德蒙的坏家伙。恰巧里根的丈夫死了，里根立刻宣布要和埃德蒙结婚。这引起了姐姐的嫉妒，她设法毒死了里根。这个阴谋被贡纳莉的丈夫发现了，他把贡纳莉关进了监牢，然而不久贡纳莉也自杀了。

科迪莉亚也没有得到更幸运的下场，她带领的军队被埃德蒙的军队打败了，科迪莉亚落入了埃德蒙的监狱，最后也被害死了。不久以后，李尔也死了。忠心的肯特很想让老国王知道自己和凯厄斯是同一个人，无奈国王发疯了，很快肯特也随着老国王走进了坟墓。那个叫做埃德蒙的坏家伙后来死于一次决斗，得到了应有的惩罚。贡纳莉的丈夫并没有参与害死科迪莉亚的恶行，也没有鼓励自己的妻子虐待父亲，李尔死后，他就做了不列颠的国王。

人物事件词汇表

Britain	不列颠 即英国
Lear	李尔 不列颠国王，故事的主人公
France	法兰西 即法国
Burgundy	勃艮第 西欧历史地区名，各历史时期所指各异。多用指除十七和十八世纪法国勃艮第省外，另拥有其他广大领土的两个王国和一个公国
Goneril	贡纳莉 李尔的大女儿
Albany	奥尔巴尼 公爵，李尔王的大女婿
Regan	里根 李尔的二女儿
Cornwall	康沃尔 公爵，李尔王的二女婿
Cordelia	科迪莉亚 李尔的三女儿
Kent	肯特 不列颠的朝臣，对李尔王忠心耿耿。后来化名凯厄斯跟在李尔王身边
Caius	凯厄斯 肯特乔装打扮的跟随在李尔王身边的仆从所用的化名
Edmund	埃德蒙 李尔王大女儿和二女儿共同的情人，一个奸诈的人

Lear, king of Britain, had three daughters; Goneril, wife to the duke of Albany; Regan, wife to the duke of Cornwall; and Cordelia, a young maid, for whose love the king of France and duke of Burgundy were joint suitors, and were at this time making stay for that purpose in the court of Lear.

The old king, worn out with age and the fatigues of government, he being more than fourscore years old, determined to take no further part in state affairs, but to leave the management to younger strengths, that he might have time to prepare for death, which must at no long period ensue. With this intent he called his three daughters to him, to know from their own lips which of them loved him best, that he might part his kingdom among them in such proportions as their affection for him should seem to deserve.

Goneril, the eldest, declared that she loved her father more than words could give out, that he was dearer to her than the light of her own eyes, dearer than life and liberty, with a deal of such professing stuff, which is easy to counterfeit where there is no real love, only a few fine words delivered with confidence being wanted in that case. The king, delighted to hear from her own mouth this assurance of her love, and thinking truly that her heart went with it, in a fit of fatherly fondness bestowed upon her and her husband one-third of his ample kingdom.

Then calling to him his second daughter, he demanded what she had to say. Regan, who was made of the same hollow metal as her sister, was not a whit behind in her profession, but rather declared that what her sister had spoken came short of the love which she professed to bear for his highness; insomuch that she found all other joys dead, in comparison with the pleasure which she took in the love of her dear king and father.

Lear blessed himself in having such loving children, as he thought; and could do no less, after the handsome assurances which Regan had made, than bestow a third of his kingdom upon her and her husband, equal in size to that which he had already given away to Goneril.

Then turning to his youngest daughter Cordelia, whom he called his joy, he asked what she had to say, thinking no doubt that she would glad his ears with the same loving speeches which her sisters had uttered, or rather that her expressions would be so much stronger than theirs, as she had always been his darling, and favoured by him above either of them. But Cordelia, disgusted with the flattery of her sisters, whose hearts she knew were far from their lips, and seeing that all their coaxing speeches were only intended to wheedle the old king out of his dominions, that they and their husbands might reign in his lifetime, made no other reply but this, that she loved his majesty according to her duty, neither more nor less.

李尔王和小女儿

科迪莉亚被父亲冷落

The king, shocked with this appearance of ingratitude in his favourite child, desired her to consider her words, and to mend her speech, lest it should mar her fortunes.

Cordelia then told her father, that he was her father, that he had given her breeding, and loved her; that she returned those duties back as was most fit, and did obey him, love him, and most honour him. But that she could not frame her mouth to such large speeches as her sisters had done, or promise to love nothing else in the world. Why had her sisters husbands, if (as they said) they had no love for anything but their father? If she should ever wed, she was sure the lord to whom she gave her hand would want half her love, half of her care and duty; she should never marry like her sisters, to love her father all.

Cordelia, who in earnest loved her old father even almost as extravagantly as her sisters pretended to do, would have plainly told him so at any other time, in more daughter-like and loving terms, and without these qualifications, which did indeed sound a little ungracious; but after the crafty flattering speeches of her sisters, which she had seen drawn such extravagant rewards, she thought the handsomest thing she could do was to love and be silent. This put her affection out of suspicion of mercenary ends, and showed that she loved, but not for gain; and that her professions, the less ostentatious they were, had so much the more of truth and sincerity than her sisters'.

This plainness of speech, which Lear called pride, so enraged the old monarch who in his best of times always showed much of spleen and rashness, and in whom the dotage incident to old age had so clouded over his reason, that he could not discern truth from flattery, nor a gay painted speech from words that came from the heart—that in a fury of resentment he retracted the third part of his kingdom, which yet remained, and which he had reserved for Cordelia, and gave it away from her, sharing it equally between her two sisters and their husbands, the dukes of Albany and Cornwall; whom he now called to him, and in presence of all his courtiers bestowing a coronet between them, invested them jointly with all the power, revenue, and execution of government, only retaining to himself the name of king; all the rest of royalty he resigned; with this reservation, that himself, with a hundred knights for his attendants, was to be maintained by monthly course in each of his daughters' palaces in turn.

So preposterous a disposal of his kingdom, so little guided by reason, and so much by passion, filled all his courtiers with astonishment and sorrow; but none of them had the courage to interpose between this incensed king and his wrath, except the earl of Kent, who was beginning to speak a good word for Cordelia, when the passionate Lear on pain of death commanded him to desist; but the good Kent was not so to be repelled. He had been ever loyal to Lear, whom he had honoured as a king, loved as a father, followed as a master; and he had never esteemed his life further than as a pawn to wage against his royal master's enemies, nor feared to lose it when Lear's safety was the motive; nor now that Lear was most his own enemy, did this faithful servant of the king forget his old principles, but manfully opposed Lear, to do Lear good; and was unmannerly only because Lear was mad. He had been a most faithful counsellor in times past to the king, and he besought him now, that he would see with his eyes (as he had done in many weighty matters), and go by his advice still; and in his best consideration recall this hideous rashness: for he would answer with his life, his judgment that Lear's youngest daughter did not love him least, nor were those empty-hearted whose low sound gave no token of hollowness. When power bowed to flattery, honour was bound to plainness. For Lear's threats, what could he do to him, whose life was already at his service? That should not hinder duty from speaking.

The honest freedom of this good earl of Kent only stirred up the king's wrath the more, and like a frantic patient who kills his physician, and loves his mortal disease, he banished this true servant, and allotted him but five days to make his preparations for departure; but if on the sixth his hated person was found within the realm of Britain, that moment was to be his death. And Kent bade farewell to the king, and said, that since he chose to show himself in such fashion, it was but banishment to stay there; and before he went, he recommended Cordelia to the protection of the gods, the maid who had so rightly thought, and so discreetly spoken; and only wished that her sisters' large speeches might be answered with deeds of love; and then he went, as he said, to shape his old course to a new country.

The king of France and duke of Burgundy were now called in to hear the determination of Lear about his youngest daughter, and to know whether they would persist in their courtship to Cordelia, now that she was under her father's displeasure, and had no fortune but her own person to recommend her: and the duke of Burgundy declined the match, and would not take her to wife upon such conditions; but the king of France, understanding what the nature of the fault had been which had lost her the love of her father, that it was only a tardiness of speech, and the not being able to frame her tongue to flattery like her sisters, took this young maid by the hand, and saying that her virtues were a dowry above a kingdom, bade Cordelia to take farewell of her sisters and of her father, though he had been unkind, and she should go with him, and be queen of him and of fair France, and reign over fairer possessions than her sisters: and he called the duke of Burgundy in contempt a waterish duke, because his love for this young maid had in a moment run all away like water.

Then Cordelia with weeping eyes took leave of her sisters, and besought them to love their father well, and make good their professions: and they sullenly told her not to prescribe to them, for they knew their duty; but to strive to content her husband, who had taken her (as they tauntingly expressed it) as Fortune's alms. And Cordelia with a heavy heart departed, for she knew the cunning of her sisters, and she wished her father in better hands than she was about to leave him in.

Cordelia was no sooner gone, than the devilish dispositions of her sisters began to show themselves in their true colours. Even before the expiration of the first month, which Lear was to spend by agreement with his eldest daughter Goneril, the old king began to find out the difference between promises and performances. This wretch having got from her father all that he had to bestow, even to the giving away of the crown from off his head, began to grudge even those small remnants of royalty which the old man had reserved to himself, to please his fancy with the idea of being still a king. She could not bear to see him and his hundred knights. Every time she met her father, she put on a frowning countenance; and when the old man wanted to speak with her, she would feign sickness, or anything to get rid of the sight of him; for it was plain that she esteemed his old age a useless burden, and his attendants an unnecessary expense: not only she herself slackened in her expressions of duty to the king, but by her example, and (it is to be feared) not without her private instructions, her very servants affected to treat him with neglect, and would either refuse to obey his orders, or still more contemptuously pretend not to hear them. Lear could not but perceive this alteration in the behaviour of his daughter, but he shut his eyes against it as long as he could, as people commonly are unwilling to believe the unpleasant consequences which their own mistakes and obstinacy have brought upon them.

True love and fidelity are no more to be estranged by ill, than falsehood and hollow-heartedness can be conciliated by good, usage. This eminently appears in the instance of the good earl of Kent, who, though banished by Lear, and his life made forfeit if he were found in Britain, chose to stay and abide all

扮成仆人的肯特

consequences, as long as there was a chance of his being useful to the king his master. See to what mean shifts and disguises poor loyalty is forced to submit sometimes; yet it counts nothing base or unworthy, so as it can but do service where it owes an obligation! In the disguise of a serving man, all his greatness and pomp laid aside, this good earl proffered his services to the king, who, not knowing him to be Kent in that disguise, but pleased with a certain plainness, or rather bluntness in his answers, which the earl put on (so different from that smooth oily flattery which he had so much reason to be sick of, having found the effects not answerable in his daughter), a bargain was quickly struck, and Lear took Kent into his service by the name of Caius, as he called himself, never suspecting him to be his once great favourite, the high and mighty earl of Kent.

This Caius quickly found means to show his fidelity and love to his royal master: for Goneril's steward that same day behaving in a disrespectful manner to Lear, and giving him saucy looks and language, as no doubt he was secretly encouraged to do by his mistress, Caius, not enduring to hear so open an affront put upon his majesty, made no more ado but presently tripped up his heels, and laid the unmannerly slave in the kennel; for which friendly service Lear became more and more attached to him.

Nor was Kent the only friend Lear had. In his degree, and as far as so insignificant a personage could show his love, the poor fool, or jester, that had been of his palace while Lear had a palace, as it was the custom of kings and great personages at that time to keep a fool (as he was called) to make them sport after serious business: this poor fool clung to Lear after he had given away his crown, and by his witty sayings would keep up his good humour, though he could not refrain sometimes from jeering at his master for his imprudence in uncrowning himself, and giving all away to his daughters; at which time, as he rhymingly expressed it, these daughters

For sudden joy did weep
And he for sorrow sung,
That such a king should play bo-peep
And go the fools among.

And in such wild sayings, and scraps of songs, of which he had plenty, this pleasant honest fool poured out his heart even in the presence of Goneril herself, in many a bitter taunt and jest which cut to the quick: such as comparing the king to the hedge-sparrow, who feeds the young of the cuckoo till they grow old enough, and then has its head bit off for its pains; and saying, that an ass may know when the cart draws the horse (meaning that Lear's daughters, that ought to go behind, now ranked before their father); and that Lear was no longer Lear, but the shadow of Lear: for which free speeches he was once or twice threatened to be whipped.

The coolness and falling off of respect which Lear had begun to perceive, were not all which this foolish fond father was to suffer from his unworthy daughter: she now plainly told him that his staying in her palace was inconvenient so long as he insisted upon keeping up an establishment of a hundred knights; that this establishment was useless and expensive, and only served to kill her court with riot and feasting; and she prayed him that he would lessen their number, and keep none but old men about him, such as himself, and fitting his age.

Lear at first could not believe his eyes or ears, nor that it was his daughter who spoke so unkindly. He could not believe that she who had received a crown from him could seek to cut off his train, and grudge him the respect due to his old age. But she persisting in her undutiful demand, the old man's rage was so excited, that he called her a detested kite, and said that she spoke an untruth; and so indeed she did, for the hundred knights were all men of choice behaviour and sobriety of manners, skilled in all particulars of duty, and not given to rioting or feasting, as she said. And he bid his horses to be prepared, for he would go to his other daughter, Regan, he and his hundred knights; and he spoke of ingratitude, and said it was a marble-hearted devil, and showed more hideous in a child than the sea-monster. And he cursed his eldest daughter Goneril so as was terrible to hear; praying that she might never have a child, or if she had, that it might live to return that scorn and contempt upon her which she had shown to him that she might feel how sharper than a serpent's tooth it was to have a thankless child. And Goneril's husband, the duke of Albany, beginning to excuse himself for any share which Lear might suppose he had in the unkindness, Lear would not hear him out, but in a rage ordered his horses to be saddled, and set out with his followers for the abode of Regan, his other daughter. And Lear thought to himself how small the fault of Cordelia (if it was a fault) now appeared, in comparison with her sister's, and he wept; and then he was ashamed that such a creature as Goneril should have so much power over his manhood as to make him weep.

Regan and her husband were keeping their court in great pomp and state at their palace; and Lear despatched his servant Caius with letters to his daughter, that she might be prepared for his reception, while he and his train followed after. But it seems that Goneril had been beforehand with him, sending letters also to Regan, accusing her father of waywardness and ill humours, and advising her not to receive so great a train as he was bringing with him. This messenger arrived at the same time with Caius, and Caius and he met: and who should it be but Caius's old enemy the steward, whom he had formerly tripped up by the heels for his saucy behaviour to Lear. Caius not liking the fellow's look, and suspecting what he came for, began to revile him, and challenged him to fight, which the fellow refusing, Caius, in a fit of honest passion, beat him soundly, as such a mischief-maker and carrier of wicked messages deserved; which coming to the ears of Regan and her husband, they ordered Caius to be put in the stocks, though he was a messenger from the king her father, and in that character demanded the highest respect: so that the first thing the king saw when he entered the castle, was his faithful servant Caius sitting in that disgraceful situation.

This was but a bad omen of the reception which he was to expect; but a worse followed, when, upon inquiry for his daughter and her husband, he was told they were weary with travelling all night, and could not see him; and when lastly, upon his insisting in a positive and angry manner to see them, they came to greet him, whom should he see in their company but the hated Goneril, who had come to tell her own story, and set her sister against the king her father!

This sight much moved the old man, and still more to see Regan take her by the hand; and he asked Goneril if she was not ashamed to look upon his old white beard. And Regan advised him to go home again with Goneril, and live with her peaceably, dismissing half of his attendants, and to ask her forgiveness; for he was old and wanted discretion, and must be ruled and led by persons that had more discretion than himself. And Lear showed how preposterous that would sound, if he were to go down on his knees, and beg of his own daughter for food and raiment, and he argued against such an unnatural dependence, declaring his resolution never to return with her, but to stay where he was with Regan, he and his hundred knights; for he said that she had not forgot the half of the kingdom which he had endowed her with, and that her eyes were not fierce like Goneril's, but mild and kind. And he said that rather than return to Goneril, with half his train cut off, he would go over to France, and beg a wretched pension of the king there, who had married his youngest daughter without a portion.

But he was mistaken in expecting kinder treatment of Regan than he had experienced from her sister Goneril. As if willing to outdo her sister in unequal behaviour, she declared that she thought fifty knights too many to wait upon him: that five-and-twenty were enough. Then Lear, nigh heart-broken, turned to Goneril and said that he would go back with her, for her fifty doubled five-and-twenty, and so her love was twice as much as Regan's. But Goneril excused herself, and said, what need of so many as five-and-twenty? or even ten? or five? when he might be waited upon by her servants, or her sister's servants? So these two wicked daughters, as if they strove to exceed each other in cruelty to their old father, who had been so good to them, by little and little would have abated him of all his train, all respect (little enough for him that once commanded a kingdom), which was left him to show that he had once been a king! Not that a splendid train is essential to happiness, but from a king to a beggar is a hard change, from commanding millions to be without one attendant; and it was the ingratitude in his daughters' denying it, more than what he would suffer by the want of it, which pierced this poor king to the heart; insomuch, that with this double ill-usage, a vexation for having so foolishly given away a kingdom, his wits began to be unsettled, and while he said he knew not what, he vowed revenge against those unnatural hags, and to make examples of them that should be a terror to the earth!

While he was thus idly threatening what his weak arm could never execute, night came on, and a loud storm of thunder and lightning with rain; and his daughters still persisting in their resolution not to admit his followers, he called for his horses, and chose rather to encounter the utmost fury of the storm abroad, than stay under the same roof with these ungrateful daughters: and they, saying that the injuries which wilful men procure to themselves are their just punishment, suffered him to go in that condition and shut their doors upon him.

李尔王被女儿赶了出来

The wind were high, and the rain and storm increased, when the old man sallied forth to combat with the elements, less sharp than his daughters' unkindness. For many miles about there was scarce a bush; and there upon a heath, exposed to the fury of the storm in a dark night, did king Lear wander out, and defy the winds and the thunder; and he bid the winds to blow the earth into the sea, or swell the waves of the sea till they drowned the earth, that no token might remain of any such ungrateful animal as man. The old king was now left with no other companion than the poor fool, who still abided with him, with his merry conceits striving to outjest misfortune, saying it was but a naughty night to swim in, and truly the king had better go in and ask his daughter's blessing:

But he that has a little tiny wit
With heigh ho, the wind and the rain!
Must make content with his fortunes fit
Though the rain it raineth every day:

and swearing it was a brave night to cool a lady's pride.

Thus poorly accompanied, this once great monarch was found by his ever-faithful servant the good earl of Kent, now transformed to Caius, who ever followed close at his side, though the king did not know him to be the earl; and he said: 'Alas! sir, are you here? creatures that love night, love not such nights as these. This dreadful storm has driven the beasts to their hiding places. Man's nature cannot endure the affliction or the fear.' And Lear rebuked him and said, these lesser evils were not felt, where a greater malady was taxed. When the mind is at ease, the body has leisure to be delicate, but the temper in his mind did take all feeling else from his senses, but of that which beat at his heart. And he spoke of filial ingratitude, and said it was all one as if the mouth should tear the hand for lifting food to it; for parents were hands and food and everything to children.

But the good Caius still persisting in his entreaties that the king would not stay out in the open air, at last persuaded him to enter a little wretched hovel which stood upon the heath, where the fool first entering, suddenly ran back terrified, saying that he had seen a spirit. But upon examination this spirit proved to be nothing more than a poor Bedlam beggar, who had crept into this deserted hovel for shelter, and with his talk about devils frighted the fool, one of those poor lunatics who are either mad, or feign to be so, the better to extort charity from the compassionate country people, who go about the country, calling themselves poor Tom and poor Turlygood, saying: 'Who gives anything to poor Tom?' sticking pins and nails and sprigs of rosemary into their arms to make them bleed; and with such horrible actions, partly by prayers, and partly with lunatic curses, they move or terrify the ignorant countryfolks into giving them alms. This poor fellow was such a one; and the king seeing him in so wretched a plight, with nothing but a blanket about his loins to cover his nakedness, could not be persuaded but that the fellow was some father who had given all away to his daughters, and brought himself to that pass: for nothing he thought could bring a man to such wretchedness but the having unkind daughters.

And from this and many such wild speeches which he uttered, the good Caius plainly perceived that he was not in his perfect mind, but that his daughters' ill usage had really made him go mad. And now the loyalty of this worthy earl of Kent showed itself in more essential services than he had hitherto found opportunity to perform. For with the assistance of some of the king's attendants who remained loyal, he had the person of his royal master removed at daybreak to the castle of Dover, where his own friends and influence, as earl of Kent, chiefly lay; and himself embarking for France, hastened to the court of Cordelia, and did there in such moving terms represent the pitiful condition of her royal father, and set out in such lively colours the inhumanity of her sisters, that this good and loving child with many tears besought the king her husband that he would give her leave to embark for England, with a sufficient power to subdue these cruel daughters and their husbands, and restore the old king her father to his throne; which being granted, she set forth, and with a royal army landed at Dover.

Lear having by some chance escaped from the guardians which the good earl of Kent had put over him to' take care of him in his lunacy, was found by some of Cordelia's train, wandering about the fields near Dover, in a pitiable condition, stark mad, and singing aloud to himself with a crown upon his head which he had made of straw, and nettles, and other wild weeds that he had picked up in the corn-fields. By the advice of the physicians, Cordelia, though earnestly desirous of seeing her father, was prevailed upon to put off the meeting, till by sleep and the operation of herbs which they gave him, he should be restored to greater composure. By the aid of these skilful physicians, to whom Cordelia promised all her gold and jewels for the recovery of the old king, Lear was soon in a condition to see his daughter.

A tender sight it was to see the meeting between this father and daughter; to see the struggles between the joy of this poor old king at beholding again his once darling child, and the shame at receiving such filial kindness from her whom he had cast off for so small a fault in his displeasure; both these passions struggling with the remains of his malady, which in his half-crazed brain sometimes made him that he scarce remembered where he was, or who it was that so kindly kissed him and spoke to him; and then he would beg the standers-by not to laugh at him, if he were mistaken in thinking this lady to be his daughter Cordelia! And then to see him fall on his knees to beg pardon of his child; and she, good lady, kneeling all the while to ask a blessing of him, and telling him that it did not become him to kneel, but it was her duty, for she was his child, his true and very child Cordial! and she kissed him (as she said) to kiss away all her sisters' unkindness, and said that they might be ashamed of themselves, to turn their old kind father with his white beard out into the cold air, when her enemy's dog, though it had bit her (as she prettily expressed it), should have stayed by her fire such a night as that, and warmed himself. And she told her father how she had come from France with purpose to bring him assistance; and he said that she must forget and forgive, for he was old and foolish, and did not know what he did, but that to be sure she had great cause not to love him, but her sisters had none. And Cordelia said that she had no cause, no more than they had.

So we will leave this old king in the protection of his dutiful and loving child, where, by the help of sleep and medicine, she and her physicians at length succeeded in winding up the untuned and jarring senses which the cruelty of his other daughters had so violently shaken. Let us return to say a word or two about those cruel daughters.

These monsters of ingratitude, who had been so false to their old father, could not be expected to prove more faithful to their own husbands. They soon grew tired of paying even the appearance of duty and affection, and in an open way showed they had fixed their loves upon another. It happened that the object of their guilty loves was the same. It was Edmund, a natural son of the late earl of Gloucester, who by his treacheries had succeeded in disinheriting his brother Edgar, the lawful heir, from his earldom, and by his wicked practices was now earl himself; a wicked man, and a fit object for the love of such wicked creatures as Goneril and Regan. It falling out about this time that the duke of Cornwall, Regan's husband, died, Regan immediately declared her intention of wedding this earl of Gloucester, which rousing the jealousy of her sister, to whom as

在监狱里

well as to Regan this wicked earl had at sundry times professed love, Goneril found means to make away with her sister by poison; but being detected in her practices, and imprisoned by her husband, the duke of Albany, for this deed, and for her guilty passion for the earl which had come to his ears, she, in a fit of disappointed love and rage, shortly put an end to her own life. Thus' the justice of Heaven at last overtook these wicked daughters.

While the eyes of all men were upon this event, admiring the justice displayed in their deserved deaths, the same eyes were suddenly taken off from this sight to admire at the mysterious ways of the same power in the melancholy fate of the young and virtuous daughter, the lady Cordelia, whose good deeds did seem to deserve a more fortunate conclusion: but it is an awful truth, that innocence and piety are not always successful in this world. The forces which Goneril and Regan had sent out under the command of the bad earl of Gloucester were victorious, and Cordelia, by the practices of this wicked earl, who did not like that any should stand between him and the throne, ended her life in prison. Thus, Heaven took this innocent lady to itself in her young years, after showing her to the world an illustrious example of filial duty. Lear did not long survive this kind child.

Before he died, the good earl of Kent, who had still attended his old master's steps from the first of his daughters' ill usage to this sad period of his decay, tried to make him understand that it was he who had followed him under the name of Caius; but Lear's care-crazed brain at that time could not comprehend how that could be, or how Kent and Caius could be the same person: so Kent thought it needless to trouble him with explanations at such a time; and Lear soon after expiring, this faithful servant to the king, between age and grief for his old master's vexations, soon followed him to the grave.

How the judgment of Heaven overtook the bad earl of Gloucester, whose treasons were discovered, and himself slain in single combat with his brother, the lawful earl; and how Goneril's husband, the duke of Albany, who was innocent of the death of Cordelia, and had never encouraged his lady in her wicked proceedings against her father, ascended the throne of Britain after the death of Lear, is needless here to narrate; Lear and his Three Daughters being dead, whose adventures alone concern our story.

麦克白

Macbeth

导读

麦克白是一个苏格兰显赫的爵士，他在战场上机智勇敢。最近，他打败了一支由挪威人援助的叛军。

麦克白和班科得胜归来。在路上遇到了三个女巫。女巫告诉麦克白，他会得到更荣耀的爵位，甚至成为国王。她们又告诉班科，他虽然比麦克白低微，但是比麦克白有福气，他的子子孙孙都会成为苏格兰的国王。

正当他们感到惊奇的时候，国王的信使带来了命令，给麦克白加封了更高位的爵士。这跟女巫的预言完全一致。麦克白满心盼望着女巫的预言能够实现，自己能够成为国王。

班科劝麦克白不要过分期待，这可能会让他做出后果严重的事。但是麦克白没有听从劝告，一心想着做国王的事。

麦克白把女巫的预言告诉了妻子。他的妻子是一个野心勃勃的人，她怂恿麦克白，要想实现愿望，就要谋杀国王。

国王到麦克白家中拜访，麦克白的妻子殷勤地接待了国王一行。晚上，国王安寝了，麦克白的夫人准备谋害国王。她灌醉了国王的侍从，拿着尖刀来到国王床前。她突然发现国王很像自己的父亲，这么一来，她就失去了动手的勇气。她回去和丈夫商量。麦克白觉得国王是一个好国王，不应该被自己杀死。麦克白的妻子在丈夫耳边不停地念叨，她不断地向自己的丈夫灌输，做事情要坚持到底，要求麦克白立刻去杀掉国王。

麦克白心中怀着恐惧杀死了国王，但恐惧让他产生了许多幻觉，他仿佛听到有个声音在说话，麦克白再也无法睡觉了。

早晨，大家发现国王被谋杀了。所有人都怀疑是麦克白做的，因为只有他能够获得最大的好处。

王位本来应该由国王的儿子继承，可是他们都逃走了。于是麦克白加冕做了国王。女巫的预言都应验了。

麦克白做了国王，他开始担心女巫预言班科的子女会成为国王也会成为现实。于是他设计要杀死班科父子。结果班科被杀死了，班科的儿子逃走了。后来班科的儿子真的做了苏格兰的国王。

就在麦克白庆祝杀死班科的宴会上，班科的鬼魂出现了。麦克白被鬼魂吓得浑身发抖。客人们都看不到鬼魂，只有麦克白一个人在和鬼魂说着话。大家都以为他疯了。麦克白的妻子赶忙送走了客人。鬼魂搅得麦克白夫妇生活不宁，而班科逃走的儿子更是让他们的内心充满了焦虑。于是，麦克白决定去寻找女巫，询问女巫未来究竟是什么样子的。

麦克白在山洞里找到了女巫。她们召唤出了三个鬼魂。第一个鬼魂告诉麦克白要当心费弗爵士。第二个鬼魂告诉麦克白凡是女人生出来的凡人的力量都不能伤害他。第三个鬼魂告诉麦克白，说他永远不会被打败，除非柏南的树林会挪到丹西嫩山来攻打麦克白。麦克白放心了。

走出山洞，麦克白听说费弗爵士参加了反抗他的军队。他一怒之下派兵杀死了爵士的妻儿。

麦克白越来越残暴，所有人都害怕他，没有人愿意为他打仗。而反抗他的军队势力越来越大。更加不幸的是，王后死了。这个麦克白阴谋的唯一同谋因为无法忍受内心的折磨，自尽了。

但是因为坚信女巫的预言，麦克白要带着军队去战斗。有一天，传令兵慌张地告诉他，好像柏南的树林挪动起来了。这让麦克白的决心开始动摇了。麦克白带领军队冲向敌人。在战场上，他遇到了费弗爵士，当他得知费弗爵士并非是从娘胎中生出来的，这让他失去了勇气。他大声地咒骂女巫。在绝望中，麦克白鼓起勇气扑向了费弗爵士，最后麦克白被砍掉了脑袋。老国王流亡在外的儿子又回国继承了王位。

人物事件词汇表

Scotland	苏格兰 是大不列颠与北爱尔兰联合王国下属的王国之一
Norway	挪威 北欧国家位于斯堪的纳维亚半岛西部，东与瑞典接壤，西邻大西洋
Macbeth	麦克白 故事的主人公，苏格兰爵士
Banquo	班科 苏格兰将军，后被麦克白杀死
Fife	费弗 爵位封号，费弗爵士是麦克白所嫉妒的人
Birnam	柏南 苏格兰的一片森林所在地
Dunsinane	丹西嫩山 苏格兰的一座山

When Duncan the Meek reigned king of Scotland, there lived a great thane, or lord, called Macbeth. This Macbeth was a near kinsman to the king, and in great esteem at court for his velour and conduct in the wars; an example of which he had lately given, in defeating a rebel army assisted by the troops of Norway in terrible numbers.

The two Scottish generals, Macbeth and Banquo, returning victorious from this great battle, their way lay over a blasted heath, where they were stopped by the strange appearance of three figures like women, except that they had beards, and their withered skins and wild attire made them look not like any earthly creatures. Macbeth first addressed them, when they, seemingly offended, laid each one her choppy finger upon her skinny lips, in token of silence; and the first of them saluted Macbeth with the title of thane of Glamis. The general was not a little startled to find himself known by such creatures; but how much more, when the second of them followed up that salute by giving him the title of thane of Cawdor, to which honour he had no pretensions; and again the third bid him 'All hail! king that shalt be hereafter!' Such a prophetic greeting might well amaze him, who knew that while the king's sons lived he could not hope to succeed to the throne. Then turning to Banquo, they pronounced him, in a sort of riddling terms, to be lesser than Macbeth and greater! not so happy, but much happier! and prophesied that though he should never reign, yet his sons after him should be kings in Scotland. They then turned into air, and vanished: by which the generals knew them to be the weird sisters, or witches.

While they stood pondering on the strangeness of this adventure, there arrived certain messengers from the king, who were empowered by him to confer upon Macbeth the dignity of thane of Cawdor: an event so miraculously corresponding with the prediction of the witches astonished Macbeth, and he stood wrapped in amazement, unable to make reply to the messengers; and in that point of time swelling hopes arose in his mind that the prediction of the third witch might in like manner have its accomplishment, and that he should one day reign king in Scotland.

Turning to Banquo, he said: 'Do you not hope that your children shall be kings, when what the witches promised to me has so wonderfully come to pass?' 'That hope,' answered the general, 'might enkindle you to aim at the throne; but oftentimes these ministers of darkness tell us truths in little things, to betray us into deeds of greatest consequence.'

But the wicked suggestions of the witches had sunk too deep into the mind of Macbeth to allow him to attend to the warnings of the good Banquo. From that time he bent all his thoughts how to compass the throne of Scotland.

Macbeth had a wife, to whom he communicated the strange prediction of the weird sisters, and its partial accomplishment. She was a bad, ambitious woman, and so as her husband and herself could arrive at greatness, she cared not much by what means. She spurred on the reluctant purpose of Macbeth, who felt compunction at the thoughts of blood, and did not cease to represent the murder of the king as a step absolutely necessary to the fulfilment of the flattering prophecy.

It happened at this time that the king, who out of his royal condescension would oftentimes visit his principal nobility upon gracious terms, came to Macbeth's house, attended by his two sons, Malcolm and Donalbain, and a numerous train of thanes and attendants, the more to honour Macbeth for the triumphal success of his wars.

The castle of Macbeth was pleasantly situated, and the air about it was sweet and wholesome, which appeared by the nests which the martlet, or swallow, had built under all the jutting friezes and buttresses of the building, wherever it found a place of advantage; for where those birds most breed and haunt, the air is observed to be delicate. The king entered well-pleased with the place, and not less so with the attentions and respect of his honoured hostess, lady Macbeth, who had the art of covering treacherous purposes with smiles; and could look like the innocent flower, while she was indeed the serpent under it.

The king being tired with his journey, went early to bed, and in his stateroom two grooms of his chamber (as was the custom) slept beside him. He had been unusually pleased with his reception, and had made presents before he retired to his principal officers; and among the rest, had sent a rich diamond to lady Macbeth, greeting her by the name of his most kind hostess.

Now was the middle of night, when over half the world nature seems dead, and wicked dreams abuse men's minds asleep, and none but the wolf and the murderer is abroad. This was the time when lady Macbeth waked to plot the murder of the king. She would not have undertaken a deed so abhorrent to her sex, but that she feared her husband's nature, that it was too full of the milk of human kindness, to do a contrived murder. She knew him to be ambitious, but withal to be scrupulous, and not yet prepared for that height of crime which commonly in the end accompanies inordinate ambition. She had won him to consent to the murder, but she doubted his resolution; and she feared that the natural tenderness of his disposition (more humane than her own) would come between, and defeat the purpose. So with her own hands armed with a dagger, she approached the king's bed; having taken care to ply the grooms of his chamber so with wine, that they slept intoxicated, and careless of their charge. There lay Duncan in a sound sleep after the fatigues of his journey, and as she viewed him earnestly, there was something in his face, as he slept, which resembled her own father; and she had not the courage to proceed.

She returned to confer with her husband. His resolution had begun to stagger. He considered that there were strong reasons against the deed. In the first place, he was not only a subject, but a near kinsman to the king; and he had been his host and entertainer that day, whose duty, by the laws of hospitality, it was to shut the door against his murderers, not bear the knife himself. Then he considered how just and merciful a king this Duncan had been, how clear of offence to his subjects, how loving to his nobility, and in particular to him; that such kings are the peculiar care of Heaven, and their subjects doubly bound to revenge their deaths. Besides, by the favours of the king, Macbeth stood high in the opinion of all sorts of men, and how would those honours be stained by the reputation of so foul a murder!

In these conflicts of the mind lady Macbeth found her husband inclining to the better part, and resolving to proceed no further. But she being a woman not easily shaken from her evil purpose, began to pour in at his ears words which infused a portion of her own spirit into his mind, assigning reason upon reason why he should not shrink from what he had undertaken, how easy the deed was; how soon it would be over; and how the action of one short night would give to all their nights and days to come sovereign sway and royalty! Then she threw contempt on his change of purpose, and accused him of fickleness and cowardice; and declared that she had given suck, and knew how tender it was to love the babe 'that milked her;' but she would, while it was smiling in her face, have plucked it from her breast, and dashed its brains out, if she had so sworn to do it, as he had sworn to perform that murder. Then she added, how practicable it was to lay the guilt of the deed upon the drunken sleepy grooms. And with the velour of her tongue she so chastised his sluggish resolutions, that he once more summoned up courage to the bloody business.

So, taking the dagger in his hand, he softly stole in the dark to the room where Duncan lay; and as he went, he thought he saw another dagger in the air, with the handle towards him, and on the blade and at the point of it drops of blood; but when he tried to grasp at it, it was nothing but air, a mere phantasm proceeding from his own hot and oppressed brain and the business he had in hand.

Getting rid of this fear, he entered the king's room, whom he despatched with one stroke of his dagger. Just as he had done the murder, one of the grooms, who slept in the chamber, laughed in his sleep, and the other cried: 'Murder,' which woke them both, but they said a short prayer; one of them said: 'God bless us!' and the other answered 'Amen'; and addressed themselves to sleep again. Macbeth, who stood listening to them, tried to say 'Amen,' when the fellow said 'God bless us!' but, though he had most need of a blessing, the word stuck in his throat, and he could not pronounce it.

Again he thought he heard a voice which cried: 'Sleep no more: Macbeth cloth murder sleep, the innocent sleep, that nourishes life.' Still it cried: 'Sleep no more,' to all the house. 'Glamis hath murdered sleep, and therefore Cawdor shall sleep no more. Macbeth shall sleep no more.'

With such horrible imaginations Macbeth returned to his listening wife, who began to think he had failed of his purpose, and that the deed was somehow frustrated. He came in so distracted a state, that she reproached him with his want of firmness, and sent him to wash his hands of the blood which stained them, while she took his dagger, with purpose to stain the cheeks of the grooms with blood, to make it seem their guilt.

Morning came, and with it the discovery of the murder, which could not be concealed; and though Macbeth and his lady made great show of grief, and the proofs against the grooms (the dagger being produced against them and their faces smeared with blood) were sufficiently strong, yet the entire suspicion fell upon Macbeth, whose inducements to such a deed were so much more forcible than such poor silly grooms could be supposed to have; and Duncan's two sons fled. Malcolm, the eldest, sought for refuge in the English court; and the youngest, Donalbain, made his escape to Ireland.

The king's sons, who should have succeeded him, having thus vacated the throne, Macbeth as next heir was crowned king, and thus the prediction of the weird sisters was literally accomplished.

Though placed so high, Macbeth and his queen could not forget the prophecy of the weird sisters, that, though Macbeth should be king, yet not his children, but the children of Banquo, should be kings after him. The thought of this, and that they had defiled their hands with blood, and done so great crimes, only to place the posterity of Banquo upon the throne, so rankled within them, that they determined to put to death both Banquo and his son, to make void the predictions of the weird sisters, which in their own case had been so remarkably brought to pass.

For this purpose they made a great supper, to which they invited all the chief thanes; and, among the rest, with marks of particular respect, Banquo and his son Fleance were invited. The way by which Banquo was to pass to the palace at night was beset by murderers appointed by Macbeth, who stabbed Banquo; but in the scuffle Fleance escaped. From that Fleance descended a race of monarchs who afterwards filled the Scottish throne, ending with James the Sixth of Scotland and the First of England, under whom the two crowns of England and Scotland were united.

At supper, the queen, whose manners were in the highest degree affable and royal, played the hostess with a gracefulness and attention which conciliated every one present, and Macbeth discoursed freely with his thanes and nobles, saying, that all that was honourable in the country was under his roof, if he had but his good friend Banquo present, whom yet he hoped he should rather have to chide for neglect, than to lament for any mischance. Just at these words the ghost of Banquo, whom he had caused to be murdered, entered the room and placed himself on the chair which Macbeth was about to occupy. Though Macbeth was a bold man, and one that could have faced the devil without trembling, at this horrible sight his cheeks turned white with fear, and he stood quite unmanned with his eyes fixed upon the ghost. His queen and all the nobles, who saw nothing, but perceived him gazing (as they thought) upon an empty chair, took it for a fit of distraction; and she reproached him, whispering that it was but the same fancy which made him see the dagger in the air, when he was about to kill Duncan. But Macbeth continued to see the ghost, and gave no heed to all they could say, while he addressed it with distracted words, yet so significant, that his queen, fearing the dreadful secret would be disclosed, in great haste dismissed the guests, excusing the infirmity of Macbeth as a disorder he was often troubled with.

To such dreadful fancies Macbeth was subject. His queen and he had their sleeps afflicted with terrible dreams, and the blood of Banquo troubled them not more than the escape of Fleance, whom now they looked upon as father to a line of kings who should keep their posterity out of the throne. With these miserable thoughts they found no peace, and Macbeth determined once more to seek out the weird sisters, and know from them the worst.

He sought them in a cave upon the heath, where they, who knew by foresight of his coming, were engaged in preparing their dreadful charms, by which they conjured up infernal spirits to reveal to them futurity. Their horrid ingredients were toads, bats, and serpents, the eye of a newt, and the tongue of a dog, the leg of a lizard, and the wing of the night-owl, the scale of a dragon, the tooth of a wolf, the maw of the ravenous salt-sea shark, the mummy of a witch, the root of the poisonous hemlock (this to have effect must be digged in the dark), the gall of a goat, and the liver of a Jew, with slips of the yew tree that roots itself in graves, and the finger of a dead child: all these were set on to boil in a great kettle, or cauldron, which, as fast as it grew too hot, was cooled with a baboon's blood: to these they poured in the blood of a sow that had eaten her young, and they threw into the flame the grease that had sweaten from a murderer's gibbet. By these charms they bound the infernal spirits to answer their questions.

It was demanded of Macbeth, whether he would have his doubts resolved by them, or by their masters, the spirits. He, nothing daunted by the dreadful ceremonies which he saw, boldly answered: 'Where are they? let me see them.' And they called the spirits, which were three. And the first arose in the likeness of an armed head, and he called Macbeth by name, and bid him beware of the thane of Fife; for which caution Macbeth thanked him; for Macbeth had entertained a jealousy of Macduff, the thane of Fife.

And the second spirit arose in the likeness of a bloody child, and he called Macbeth by name, and bid him have no fear, but laugh to scorn the power of man, for none of woman born should have power to hurt him; and he advised him to be bloody, bold, and resolute. 'Then live, Macduff!' cried the king; 'what need I fear of thee? but yet I will make assurance doubly sure. Thou shalt not live; that I may tell pale-hearted Fear it lies, and sleep in spite of thunder.'

That spirit being dismissed, a third arose in the form of a child crowned, with a tree in his hand. He called Macbeth by name, and comforted him against conspiracies, saying, that he should never be vanquished, until the wood of Birnam to Dunsinane Hill should come against him. 'Sweet bodements! good!' cried Macbeth; 'who can unfix the forest, and move it from its earth-bound roots? I see I shall live the usual period of man's life, and not be cut off by a violent death. But my heart throbs to know one thing. Tell me, if your art can tell so much, if Banquo's issue shall ever reign in this kingdom?' Here the cauldron sank into the ground, and a noise of music was heard, and eight shadows, like kings, passed by Macbeth, and Banquo last, who bore a glass which showed the figures of many more, and Banquo all bloody smiled upon Macbeth, and pointed to them; by which Macbeth knew that these were the posterity of Banquo, who should reign after him in Scotland; and the witches, with a sound of soft music, and with dancing, making a show of duty and welcome to Macbeth, vanished. And from this time the thoughts of Macbeth were all bloody and dreadful.

The first thing he heard when he got out of the witches' cave, was that Macduff, thane of Fife, had fled to England, to join the army which was forming against him under Malcolm, the eldest son of the late king, with intent to displace Macbeth, and set Malcolm, the right heir, upon the throne. Macbeth, stung with rage, set upon the castle of Macduff, and put his wife and children, whom the thane had left behind, to the sword, and extended the slaughter to all who claimed the least relationship to Macduff.

These and such-like deeds alienated the minds of all his chief nobility from him. Such as could, fled to join with Malcolm and Macduff, who were now approaching with a powerful army, which they had raised in England; and the rest secretly wished success to their arms, though for fear of Macbeth they could take no active part. His recruits went on slowly. Everybody hated the tyrant; nobody loved or honoured him; but all suspected him, and he began to envy the condition of Duncan, whom he had murdered, who slept soundly in his grave, against whom treason had done its worst: steel nor poison, domestic malice nor foreign levies, could hurt him any longer.

While these things were acting, the queen, who had been the sole partner in his wickedness, in whose bosom he could sometimes seek a momentary repose from those terrible dreams which afflicted them both nightly, died, it is supposed, by her own hands, unable to bear the remorse of guilt, and public hate; by which event he was left alone, without a soul to love or care for him, or a friend to whom he could confide his wicked purposes.

He grew careless of life, and wished for death, but the near approach of Malcolm's army roused in him what remained of his ancient courage, and he determined to die (as he expressed it) 'with armour on his back.' Besides this, the hollow promises of the witches had filled him with a false confidence, and he remembered the sayings of the spirits, that none of woman born was to hurt him, and that he was never to be vanquished till Birnam wood should come to Dunsinane, which he thought could never be. So he shut himself up in his castle, whose impregnable strength was such as defied a siege: here he sullenly waited the approach of Malcolm. When, upon a day, there came a messenger to him, pale and shaking with fear, almost unable to report that which he had seen; for he averred, that as he stood upon his watch on the hill, he looked towards Birnam, and to his thinking the wood began to move! 'Liar and slave!' cried Macbeth: 'if thou speakest false, thou shalt hang alive upon the next tree, till famine end thee. If thy tale be true, I care not if thou cost as much by me': for Macbeth now began to faint in resolution, and to doubt the equivocal speeches of the spirits. He was not to fear till Birnam wood should come to Dunsinane; and now a wood did move! 'However,' said he, 'if this which he avouches be true, let us arm and out. There is no flying hence, nor staying here. I begin to be weary of the sun, and wish my life at an end.' With these desperate speeches he sallied forth upon the besiegers, who had now come up to the castle.

The strange appearance which had given the messenger an idea of a wood moving is easily solved. When the besieging army marched through the wood of Birnam, Malcolm, like a skilful general, instructed his soldiers to hew down every one a bough and bear it before him, by way of concealing the true numbers of his host. This marching of the soldiers with boughs had at a distance the appearance which had frightened the messenger. Thus were the words of the spirit brought to pass, in a sense different from that in which Macbeth had understood them, and one great hold of his confidence was gone.

And now a severe skirmishing took place, in which Macbeth, though feebly supported by those who called themselves his friends, but in reality hated the tyrant and inclined to the party of Malcolm and Macduff, yet fought with the extreme of rage and velour, cutting to pieces all who were opposed to him, till he came to where Macduff was fighting. Seeing Macduff, and remembering the caution of the spirit who had counselled him to avoid Macduff, above all men, he would have turned, but Macduff, who had been seeking him through the whole fight, opposed his turning, and a fierce contest ensued; Macduff giving him many foul reproaches for the murder of his wife and children. Macbeth, whose soul was charged enough with blood of that family already, would still have declined the combat: but Macduff still urged him to it, calling him tyrant, murderer, hell-hound, and villain.

Then Macbeth remembered the words of the spirit, how none of woman born should hurt him; and smiling confidently he said to Macduff: 'Thou losest thy labour, Macduff. As easily thou mayest impress the air with thy sword, as make me vulnerable. I bear a charmed life, which must not yield to one of woman born.'

'Despair thy charm,' said Macduff, 'and let that lying spirit whom thou hast served, tell thee, that Macduff was never born of woman, never as the ordinary manner of men is to be born, but was untimely taken from his mother.'

'Accursed be the tongue which tells me so,' said the trembling Macbeth, who felt his last hold of confidence give way; 'and let never man in future believe the lying equivocations of witches and juggling spirits, who deceive us in words which have double senses, and while they keep their promise literally, disappoint our hopes with a different meaning. I will not fight with thee.'

'Then live!' said the scornful Macduff; 'we will have a show of thee, as men show monsters, and a painted board, on which shall be written: 'Here men may see the tyrant!"

'Never,' said Macbeth, whose courage returned with despair; 'I will not live to kiss the ground before young Malcolm's feet, and to be baited with the curses of the rabble. Though Birnam wood be come to Dunsinane, and thou opposed to me, who west never born of woman, yet will I try the last.' With these frantic words he threw himself upon Macduff, who, after a severe struggle, in the end overcame him, and cutting off his head, made a present of it to the young and lawful king, Malcolm; who took upon him the government which, by the machinations of the usurper, he had so long been deprived of, and ascended the throne of Duncan the Meek, amid the acclamations of the nobles and the people.

雅典的泰蒙

Timon of Athens

导 读

泰蒙是雅典的贵族，他拥有数不清的财富，为人很慷慨，把钱挥霍在不同人的身上，所以他的进项总也赶不上他的耗费。他拥有巨额财富，又如此慷慨，自然得到了大家的爱戴，所有人都巴结奉承泰蒙。

无论你拿来怎样无用的东西，泰蒙都会花大价钱买下来。泰蒙身边还聚集了许多浪子，他们陪着泰蒙挥霍那些不属于自己的财富，而且感到心安理得。文提狄斯就是这群人中最过分的一个。

有许多人给泰蒙送礼，而泰蒙都会大方地给出回礼，回礼的价值远远超过了礼物的价值。甚至有些人只是对泰蒙的某件物品夸赞几句，泰蒙就会把这件物品送给他们。

泰蒙也用自己的财富做了些仗义疏财的事情，然而更多的是花在了恶棍和寄生虫身上。泰蒙区分不清谄媚者和朋友，他不停地挥霍着。

他的管家是一个诚实的人。他把账本拿给泰蒙，希望泰蒙能够收敛，然而泰蒙从来都不曾理会。

终于有一天，泰蒙让管家把一部分田产卖掉去偿还债务，管家告诉泰蒙，大部分田产已经卖掉了，现在他的全部产业连一半债务都不够还。

泰蒙十分吃惊，接着他安慰管家。他相信自己过去交往的人会帮助他的。可是泰蒙在朋友那里得到的都是冷遇和白眼，没有人愿意帮助他。现在泰蒙的家里全是讨债人的身影。

就在大家都以为泰蒙已经彻底穷苦的时候，泰蒙再一次宣布要请客了。过去常来的那些人都来了。他们发现泰蒙只是装穷来测试他们的友情，于是他们都来寻求泰蒙的原谅。在宴会上，泰蒙大声地咒骂他们，把盘子扔向那些忘恩负义的人。客人们都被吓得逃离了泰蒙的家。

这是泰蒙最后一次请客了，从此他就离开了雅典，离开了有人的地方。他隐居在山里，和动物为伴，与自然为伴。一次偶然的机会，他挖到了一堆金子，正巧有一队士兵路过。泰蒙将金子都给了士兵，只要求士兵能够攻打雅典。士兵拿走了金子，并且按照他的要求做了。

雅典受到了猛烈的进攻，所有人都感到害怕了。他们跑到泰蒙的面前，请求泰蒙的原谅，他们许诺给泰蒙权力和财富，只要那些士兵不再攻击雅典了。泰蒙拒绝了这群人。

最后，人们在泰蒙隐居的洞旁发现了泰蒙的坟墓，墓前有一块儿写着泰蒙憎恨人类的墓志铭，大家不知道泰蒙是怎么死的，但是都觉得这个墓志铭写得很贴切。

人物事件词汇表

Timon　泰蒙 故事的主人公，雅典的贵族

Timon, a lord of Athens, in the enjoyment of a princely fortune, affected a humour of liberality which knew no limits. His almost infinite wealth could not flow in so fast, but he poured it out faster upon all sorts and degrees of people. Not the poor only tasted of his bounty, but great lords did not disdain to rank themselves among his dependents and followers. His table was resorted to by all the luxurious feasters, and his house was open to all comers and goers at Athens. His large wealth combined with his free and prodigal nature to subdue all hearts to his love; men of all minds and dispositions tendered their services to lord Timon, from the glass-faced flatterer, whose face reflects as in a mirror the present humour of his patron, to the rough and unbending cynic, who affecting a contempt of men's persons, and an indifference to worldly things, yet could not stand out against the gracious manners and munificent soul of lord Timon, but would come (against his nature) to partake of his royal entertainments, and return most rich in his own estimation if he had received a nod or a salutation from Timon.

If a poet had composed a work which wanted a recommendatory introduction to the world, he had no more to do but to dedicate it to lord Timon, and the poem was sure of sale, besides a present purse from the patron, and daily access to his house and table. If a painter had a picture to dispose of, he had only to take it to lord Timon, and pretend to consult his taste as to the merits of it; nothing more was wanting to persuade the liberal-hearted lord to buy it. If a jeweller had a stone of price, or a mercer rich costly stuffs, which for their costliness lay upon his hands, lord Timon's house was a ready mart always open, where they might get off their wares or their jewellery at any price, and the good-natured lord would thank them into the bargain, as if they had done him a piece of courtesy in letting him have the refusal of such precious commodities. So that by this means his house was thronged with superfluous purchases, of no use but to swell uneasy and ostentatious pomp; and his person was still more inconveniently beset with a crowd of these idle visitors, lying poets, painters, sharking tradesmen, lords, ladies, needy courtiers, and expectants, who continually filled his lobbies, raining their fulsome flatteries in whispers in his ears, sacrificing to him with adulation as to a God, making sacred the very stirrup by which he mounted his horse, and seeming as though they drank the free air but through his permission and bounty.

Some of these daily dependents were young men of birth, who (their means not answering to their extravagance) had been put in prison by creditors, and redeemed thence by lord Timon; these young prodigals thenceforward fastened upon his lordship, as if by common sympathy he were necessarily endeared to all such spendthrifts and loose livers, who, not being able to follow him in his wealth, found it easier to copy him in prodigality and copious spending of what was their own. One of these flesh-flies was Ventidius, for whose debts, unjustly contracted, Timon but lately had paid down the sum of five talents.

But among this confluence, this great flood of visitors, none were more conspicuous than the makers of presents and givers of gifts. It was fortunate for these men if Timon took a fancy to a dog or a horse, or any piece of cheap furniture which was theirs. The thing so praised, whatever it was, was sure to be sent the next morning with the compliments of the giver for lord Timon's acceptance, and apologies for the unworthiness of the gift; and this dog or horse, or whatever it might be, did not fail to produce from Timon's bounty, who would not be outdone in gifts, perhaps twenty dogs or horses, certainly presents of far richer worth, as these pretended donors knew well enough, and that their false presents were but the putting out of so much money at large and speedy interest. In this way lord Lucius had lately sent to Timon a present of four milk-white horses, trapped in silver, which this cunning lord had observed Timon upon some occasion to commend; and another lord, Lucullus, had bestowed upon him in the same pretended way of free gift a brace of greyhounds, whose make and fleetness Timon had been heard to admire; these presents the easy-hearted lord accepted without suspicion of the dishonest views of the presenters; and the givers of course were rewarded with some rich return, a diamond or some jewel of twenty times the value of their false and mercenary donation.

Sometimes these creatures would go to work in a more direct way, and with gross and palpable artifice, which yet the credulous Timon was too blind to see, would affect to admire and praise something that Timon possessed, a bargain that he had bought, or some late purchase, which was sure to draw from this yielding and soft-hearted lord a gift of the thing commended, for no service in the world done for it but the easy expense of a little cheap and obvious flattery. In this way Timon but the other day had given to one of these mean lords the bay courser which he himself rode upon, because his lordship had been pleased to say that it was a handsome beast and went well; and Timon knew that no man ever justly praised what he did not wish to possess. For lord Timon weighed his friends' affection with his own, and so fond was he of bestowing, that he could have dealt kingdoms to these supposed friends, and never have been weary.

Not that Timon's wealth all went to enrich these wicked flatterers; he could do noble and praiseworthy actions; and when a servant of his once loved the daughter of a rich Athenian, but could not hope to obtain her by reason that in wealth and rank the maid was so far above him, lord Timon freely bestowed upon his servant three Athenian talents, to make his fortune equal with the dowry which the father of the young maid demanded of him who should be her husband. But for the most part, knaves and parasites had the command of his fortune, false friends whom he did not know to be such, but, because they flocked around his person, he thought they must needs love him; and because they smiled and flattered him, he thought surely that his conduct was approved by all the wise and good. And when he was feasting in the midst of all these flatterers and mock friends, when they were eating him up, and draining his fortunes dry with large draughts of richest wines drunk to his health and prosperity, he could not perceive the difference of a friend from a flatterer, but to his deluded eyes (made proud with the sight) it seemed a precious comfort to have so many like brothers commanding one another's fortunes (though it was his own fortune which paid all the costs), and with joy they would run over at the spectacle of such, as it appeared to him, truly festive and fraternal meeting.

But while he thus outwent the very heart of kindness, and poured out his bounty, as if Plutus, the god of gold, had been but his steward; while thus he proceeded without care or stop, so senseless of expense that he would neither inquire how he could maintain it, nor cease his wild flow of riot; his riches, which were not infinite, must needs melt away before a prodigality which knew no limits. But who should tell him so? his flatterers? they had no interest in shutting his eyes. In vain did his honest steward Flavius try to represent to him his condition, laying his accounts before him, begging of him, praying of him, with an importunity that on any other occasion would have been unmannerly in a servant, beseeching him with tears to look into the state of his affairs. Timon would still put him off, and turn the discourse to something else; for nothing is so deaf to remonstrance as riches turned to poverty, nothing is so unwilling to believe its situation, nothing so incredulous to its own true state, and hard to give credit to a reverse. Often had this good steward, this honest creature, when all the rooms of Timon's great house have been choked up with riotous feeders at his master's cost, when the floors have wept with drunken spilling of wine, and every apartment has blazed with lights and resounded with music and feasting, often had he retired by himself to some solitary spot, and wept faster than the wine ran from the wasteful casks within, to see the mad bounty of his lord, and to think, when the means were gone which brought him praises from all sorts of people, how quickly the breath would be gone of which the praise was made; praises won in feasting would be lost in feasting, and at one cloud of winter-showers these flies would disappear.

But now the time was come that Timon could shut his ears no longer to the representations of this faithful steward. Money must be had; and when he ordered Flavius to sell some of his land for that purpose, Flavius informed him, what he had in vain endeavoured at several times before to make him listen to, that most of his land was already sold or forfeited, and that all he possessed at present was not enough to pay the one half of what he owed. Struck with wonder at this presentation, Timon hastily replied: 'My lands extend from Athens to Lacedaemon.' 'O my good lord,' said Flavius, 'the world is but a world, and has bounds; were it all yours to give in a breath, how quickly were it gone!'

Timon consoled himself that no villanous bounty had yet come from him, that if he had given his wealth away unwisely, it had not been bestowed to feed his vices, but to cherish his friends; and he made the kind-hearted steward (who was weeping) to take comfort in the assurance that his master could never lack means, while he had so many noble friends; and this infatuated lord persuaded himself that he had nothing to do but to send and borrow, to use every man's fortune (that had ever tasted his bounty) in this extremity, as freely as his own. Then with a cheerful look, as if confident of the trial, he severally despatched messengers to lord Lucius, to lords Lucullus and Sempronius, men upon whom he had lavished his gifts in past times without measure or moderation; and to Ventidius, whom he had lately released out of prison by paying his debts, and who, by the death of his father, was now come into the possession of an ample fortune, and well enabled to requite Timon's courtesy: to request of Ventidius the return of those five talents which he had paid for him, and of each of those noble lords the loan of fifty talents; nothing doubting that their gratitude would supply his wants (if he needed it) to the amount of five hundred times fifty talents.

Lucullus was the first applied to. This mean lord had been dreaming overnight of a silver bason and cup, and when Timon's servant was announced, his sordid mind suggested to him that this was surely a making out of his dream, and that Timon had sent him such a present: but when he understood the truth of the matter, and that Timon wanted money, the quality of his faint and watery friendship showed itself, for with many protestations he vowed to the servant that he had long foreseen the ruin of his master's affairs, and many a time had he come to dinner to tell him of it, and had come again to supper to try to persuade him to spend less, but he would take no counsel nor warning by his coming: and true it was that he had been a constant attender (as he said) at Timon's feasts, as he had in greater things tasted his bounty; but that he ever came with that intent, or gave good counsel or reproof to Timon, was a base unworthy lie, which he suitably followed up with meanly offering the servant a bribe, to go home to his master and tell him that he had not found Lucullus at home.

As little success had the messenger who was sent to lord Lucius. This lying lord, who was full of Timon's meat, and enriched almost to bursting with Timon's costly presents, when he found the wind changed, and the fountain of so much bounty suddenly stopped, at first could hardly believe it; but on its being confirmed, he affected great regret that he should not have it in his power to serve lord Timon, for unfortunately (which was a base falsehood) he had made a great purchase the day before, which had quite disfurnished him of the means at present, the more beast he, he called himself, to put it out of his power to serve so good a friend; and he counted it one of his greatest afflictions that his ability should fail him to pleasure such an honourable gentleman.

Who can call any man friend that dips in the same dish with him? just of this metal is every flatterer. In the recollection of everybody Timon had been a father to this Lucius, had kept up his credit with his purse; Timon's money had gone to pay the wages of his servants, to pay the hire of the labourers who had sweat to build the fine houses which Lucius's pride had made necessary to him: yet, oh! the monster which man makes himself when he proves ungrateful! this Lucius now denied to Timon a sum, which, in respect of what Timon had bestowed on him, was less than charitable men afford to beggars.

Sempronius, and every one of these mercenary lords to whom Timon applied in their turn, returned the same evasive answer or direct denial; even Ventidius, the redeemed and now rich Ventidius, refused to assist him with the loan of those five talents which Timon had not lent but generously given him in his distress.

Now was Timon as much avoided in his poverty as he had been courted and resorted to in his riches. Now the same tongues which had been loudest in his praises, extolling him as bountiful, liberal, and open handed, were not ashamed to censure that very bounty as folly, that liberality as profuseness, though it had shown itself folly in nothing so truly as in the selection of such unworthy creatures as themselves for its objects. Now was Timon's princely mansion forsaken, and become a shunned and hated place, a place for men to pass by, not a place, as formerly, where every passenger must stop and taste of his wine and good cheer; now, instead of being thronged with feasting and tumultuous guests, it was beset with impatient and clamorous creditors, usurers, extortioners, fierce and intolerable in their demands, pleading bonds, interest, mortgages; iron-hearted men that would take no denial nor putting off, that Timon's house was now his jail, which he could not pass, nor go in nor out for them; one demanding his due of fifty talents, another bringing in a bill of five thousand crowns, which if he would tell out his blood by drops, and pay them so, he had not enough in his body to discharge, drop by drop.

In this desperate and irremediable state (as it seemed) of his affairs, the eyes of all men were suddenly surprised at a new and incredible lustre which this setting sun put forth. Once more lord Timon proclaimed a feast, to which he invited his accustomed guests, lords, ladies, all that was great or fashionable in Athens. Lord Lucius and Lucullus came, Ventidius, Sempronius, and the rest. Who more sorry now than these fawning wretches, when they found (as they thought) that Lord Timon's poverty was all pretence, and had been only to make trial of their loves, to think that they should not have seen through the artifice at the time, and have had the cheap credit of obliging his lordship? yet who more glad to find the fountain of that noble bounty, which they had thought dried up, still fresh and running? They came dissembling, protesting, expressing deepest sorrow and shame, that when his lordship sent to them, they should have been so unfortunate as to want the present means to oblige so honourable a friend. But Timon begged them not to give such trifles a thought, for he had altogether forgotten it. And these base fawning lords, though they had denied him money in his adversity, yet could not refuse their presence at this new blaze of his returning prosperity. For the swallow follows not summer more willingly than men of these dispositions follow the good fortunes of the great, nor more willingly leaves winter than these shrink from the first appearance of a reverse; such summer birds are men. But now with music and state the banquet of smoking dishes was served up; and when the guests had a little done admiring whence the bankrupt Timon could find means to furnish so costly a feast, some doubting whether the scene which they saw was real, as scarce trusting their own eyes; at a signal given, the dishes were uncovered, and Timon's drift appeared: instead of those varieties and far-fetched dainties which they expected, that Timon's epicurean table in past times had so liberally presented, now appeared under the covers of these dishes a preparation more suitable to Timon's poverty, nothing but a little smoke and lukewarm water, fit feast for this knot of mouth-friends, whose professions were indeed smoke, and their hearts lukewarm and slippery as the water with which Timon welcomed his astonished guests, bidding them, 'Uncover, dogs, and lap'; and before they could recover their surprise, sprinkling it in their faces, that they might have enough, and throwing dishes and all after them, who now ran huddling out, lords, ladies, with their caps snatched up in haste, a splendid confusion, Timon pursuing them, still calling them what they were, 'smooth smiling parasites, destroyers under the mask of courtesy, affable wolves, meek bears, fools of fortune, feast-friends, time-flies.' They, crowding out to avoid him, left the house more willingly than they had entered it; some losing their gowns and caps, and some their jewels in the hurry, all glad to escape out of the presence of such a mad lord, and from the ridicule of his mock banquet.

This was the last feast which ever Timon made, and in it he took farewell of Athens and the society of men; for, after that, he betook himself to the woods, turning his back upon the hated city and upon all mankind, wishing the walls of that detestable city might sink, and the houses fall upon their owners, wishing all plagues which infest humanity, war, outrage, poverty, diseases, might fasten upon its inhabitants, praying the just gods to confound all Athenians, both young and old, high and low; so wishing, he went to the woods, where he said he should find the unkindest beast much kinder than mankind. He stripped himself naked, that he might retain no fashion of a man, and dug a cave to live in, and lived solitary in the manner of a beast, eating the wild roots, and drinking water, flying from the face of his kind, and choosing rather to herd with wild beasts, as more harmless and friendly than man.

What a change from lord Timon the rich, lord Timon the delight of mankind, to Timon the naked, Timon the man-hater! Where were his flatterers now? Where were his attendants and retinue? Would the bleak air, that boisterous servitor, be his chamberlain, to put his shirt on warm? Would those stiff trees that had outlived the eagle, turn young and airy pages to him, to skip on his errands when he bade them? Would the cool brook, when it was iced with winter, administer to him his warm broths and caudles when sick of an overnight's surfeit? Or would the creatures that lived in those wild woods come and lick his hand and flatter him?

Here on a day, when he was digging for roots, his poor sustenance, his spade struck against something heavy, which proved to be gold, a great heap which some miser had probably buried in a time of alarm, thinking to have come again, and taken it from its prison, but died before the opportunity had arrived, without making any man privy to the concealment; so it lay, doing neither good nor harm, in the bowels of the earth, its mother, as if it had never come from thence, till the accidental striking of Timon's spade against it once more brought it to light.

Here was a mass of treasure which, if Timon had retained his old mind, was enough to have purchased him friends and flatterers again; but Timon was sick of the false world, and the sight of gold was poisonous to his eyes; and he would have restored it to the earth, but that, thinking of the infinite calamities which by means of gold happen to mankind, how the lucre of it causes robberies, oppression, injustice, briberies, violence, and murder, among men, he had a pleasure in imagining (such a rooted hatred did he bear to his species) that out of this heap, which in digging he had discovered, might arise some mischief to plague mankind. And some soldiers passing through the woods near to his cave at that instant, which proved to be a part of the troops of the Athenian captain Alcibiades, who upon some disgust taken against the senators of Athens (the Athenians were ever noted to be a thankless and ungrateful people, giving disgust to their generals and best friends), was marching at the head of the same triumphant army which he had formerly headed in their defence, to war against them; Timon, who liked their business well, bestowed upon their captain the gold to pay his soldiers, requiring no other service from him, than that he should with his conquering army lay Athens level with the ground, and burn, slay, kill all her inhabitants; not sparing the old men for their white beards, for (he said) they were usurers, nor the young children for their seeming innocent smiles, for those (he said) would live, if they grew up, to be traitors; but to steel his eyes and ears against any sights or sounds that might awaken compassion; and not to let the cries of virgins, babes, or mothers, hinder him from making one universal massacre of the city, but to confound them all in his conquest; and when he had conquered, he prayed that the gods would confound him also, the conqueror: so thoroughly did Timon hate Athens, Athenians, and all mankind.

While he lived in this forlorn state, leading a life more brutal than human, he was suddenly surprised one day with the appearance of a man standing in an admiring posture at the door of his cave. It was Flavius, the honest steward, whom love and zealous affection to his master had led to seek him out at his wretched dwelling, and to offer his services; and the first sight of his master, the once noble Timon, in that abject condition, naked as he was born, living in the manner of a beast among beasts, looking like his own sad ruins and a monument of decay, so affected this good servant, that he stood speechless, wrapped up in horror, and confounded. And when he found utterance at last to his words, they were so choked with tears, that Timon had much ado to know him again, or to make out who it was that had come (so contrary to the experience he had had of mankind) to offer him service in extremity. And being in the form and shape of a man, he suspected him for a traitor, and his tears for false; but the good servant by so many tokens confirmed the truth of his fidelity, and made it clear that nothing but love and zealous duty to his once dear master had brought him there, that Timon was forced to confess that the world contained one honest man; yet, being in the shape and form of a man, he could not look upon his man's face without abhorrence, or hear words uttered from his man's lips without loathing; and this singly honest man was forced to depart, because he was a man, and because, with a heart more gentle and compassionate than is usual to man, he bore man's detested form and outward feature.

But greater visitants than a poor steward were about to interrupt the savage quiet of Timon's solitude. For now the day was come when the ungrateful lords of Athens sorely repented the injustice which they had done to the noble Timon. For Alcibiades, like an incensed wild boar, was raging at the walls of their city, and with his hot siege threatened to lay fair Athens in the dust. And now the memory of lord Timon's former prowess and military conduct came fresh into their forgetful minds, for Timon had been their general in past times, and a valiant and expert soldier, who alone of all the Athenians was deemed able to cope with a besieging army such as then threatened them, or to drive back the furious approaches of Alcibiades.

A deputation of the senators was chosen in this emergency to wait upon Timon. To him they come in their extremity, to whom, when he was in extremity they had shown but small regard; as if they presumed upon his gratitude whom they had disobliged, and had derived a claim to his courtesy from their own most discourteous and unpiteous treatment.

Now they earnestly beseech him, implore him with tears, to return and save that city, from which their ingratitude had so lately driven him; now they offer him riches, power, dignities, satisfaction for past injuries, and public honours, and the public love; their persons, lives, and fortunes, to be at his disposal, if he will but come back and save them. But Timon the naked, Timon the man-hater, was no longer lord Timon, the lord of bounty, the flower of velour, their defence in war, their ornament in peace. If Alcibiades killed his countrymen, Timon cared not. If he sacked fair Athens, and slew her old men and her infants, Timon would rejoice. So he told them; and that there was not a knife in the unruly camp which he did not prize above the reverendest throat in Athens.

This was all the answer he vouchsafed to the weeping disappointed senators; only at parting he bade them commend him to his countrymen, and tell them, that to ease them of their griefs and anxieties, and to prevent the consequences of fierce Alcibiades' wrath, there was yet a way left, which he would teach them, for he had yet so much affection left for his dear countrymen as to be willing to do them a kindness before his death. These words a little revived the senators, who hoped that his kindness for their city was returning. Then Timon told them that he had a tree, which grew near his cave, which he should shortly have occasion to cut down, and he invited all his friends in Athens, high or low, of what degree soever, who wished to shun affliction, to come and take a taste of his tree before he cut it down; meaning, that they might come and hang themselves on it, and escape affliction that way.

And this was the last courtesy of all his noble bounties, which Timon showed to mankind, and this the last sight of him which his countrymen had: for not many days after, a poor soldier, passing by the sea-beach, which was at a little distance from the woods which Timon frequented, found a tomb on the verge of the sea, with an inscription upon it, purporting that it was the grave of Timon the man-hater, who 'While he lived, did hate all living men, and dying wished a plague might consume all caitiffs left!'

Whether he finished his life by violence, or whether mere distaste of life and the loathing he had for mankind brought Timon to his conclusion, was not clear, yet all men admired the fitness of his epitaph, and the consistency of his end; dying, as he had lived, a hater of mankind: and some there were who fancied a conceit in the very choice which he had made of the sea-beach for his place of burial, where the vast sea might weep for ever upon his grave, as in contempt of the transient and shallow tears of hypocritical and deceitful mankind.

罗密欧与朱丽叶

Romeo and Juliet

导 读

开普莱特家和蒙泰古家是维罗纳城的两个大族。两家之间有很深的仇恨，经常会闹出流血事件。

老开普莱特大人举办了一场晚宴，邀请了许多宾客，只要不是蒙泰古家的人都是受欢迎的。老蒙泰古大人的儿子罗密欧在好友本沃利奥的怂恿下戴着面具参加了晚宴。

在宴会上，罗密欧看到了一位非常美丽的女孩子，他被她深深地吸引住了，围在这个女孩子身边不停地赞美着她。罗密欧的声音被提博尔特听出来了，他觉得有蒙泰古家的人参加了晚宴是对开普莱特家的侮辱，当时就想打死罗密欧。老开普莱特大人制止了他。

罗密欧戴着面具接近了那位美人，嘴里诉说着情话。后来姑娘的母亲把姑娘叫走了。罗密欧四处打听才知道，那姑娘正是老开普莱特大人的女儿朱丽叶；朱丽叶也被告知和她谈话的人是蒙泰古家的罗密欧。

到了半夜，罗密欧偷偷来到朱丽叶的楼下。这时偏巧朱丽叶在楼上一个人自言自语，诉说着对罗密欧的爱意。罗密欧偷听到了朱丽叶的誓言，再也按捺不住，他从阴影中走出来，向朱丽叶表达了自己的爱意。两个年轻人就这样互相倾诉着，直到奶妈来叫朱丽叶去睡觉。两人约好，明天朱丽叶会派人去见罗密欧，约定结婚的时间。这个夜晚让两个年轻人的内心充满了幸福。

分开之后，罗密欧去见了劳伦思神父，他把自己与朱丽叶的爱情都告诉了神父。神父觉得如果两个年轻人能够定下亲事的话，说不定可以化解两家的仇恨，所以他答应替两个人主持婚礼。

罗密欧

得知神父答应主持婚礼，朱丽叶也赶到了神父的密室。在那里，神父为两个年轻人举行了仪式。婚礼举行完，朱丽叶赶紧回家去。罗密欧答应晚上去和她相会。

当天中午，本沃利奥和莫丘西奥碰到了开普莱特家的提博尔特，双方吵了起来。这时罗密欧也来了。提博尔特又找罗密欧的碴儿。这会儿，罗密欧对开普莱特家已经没有仇恨了，所以非常忍让。他的朋友莫丘西奥冲上来和提博尔特交手了。两个格斗者被分开的时候，莫丘西奥被刺死了。这下子罗密欧再也忍不住了，他和提博尔特打了起来，结果提博尔特被杀死了。

这场骚乱把亲王和两家的老人都引来了。双方都要求亲王能够秉公处理。最后亲王决定把罗密欧驱逐出维罗纳。

这个消息让朱丽叶内心充满了矛盾，因为被杀死的是自己的堂兄，被放逐的是自己的丈夫。而这时候罗密欧躲在劳伦思神父的密室里，也被放逐的处罚折磨得想要自杀了。最后还是神父劝阻了他。罗密欧决定晚上去见朱丽叶，然后就到曼图阿去。

两个年轻人在一起度过了一夜。天刚亮，罗密欧就离开了。两个人心中都充满了悲伤。不过罗密欧必须得离开了。

过了没几天，老开普莱特大人为朱丽叶许了一门亲事，他并不知道自己的女儿已经成了别人的妻子。他替她挑选的丈夫是潘里斯伯爵，也是一个体面的人物。

朱丽叶用了种种理由，想要推掉这门亲事，但这都被老开普莱特大人当作了女孩子的矜持。他坚持要把女儿嫁出去。

朱丽叶找到了劳伦思神父，向神父寻求帮助。神父给了她一个小药瓶。药水能够让人在四十二小时之内僵冷、毫无知觉，然后就会醒过来。神父让朱丽叶服药后假死，然后和罗密欧一起到曼图阿去生活。

回去之后，朱丽叶就答应了潘里斯伯爵的求婚。结婚前夜，朱丽叶把药喝了下去。

第二天，大家发现朱丽叶死了，整个开普莱特家被悲伤的情绪笼罩着。而劳伦思神父还没有把计划告诉罗密欧，罗密欧就得知朱丽叶死了。他在曼图阿买了一瓶毒药，然后动身去了维罗纳。

在开普莱特家的墓地，罗密欧遇到了来悼念亡妻的潘里斯伯爵，两个人因为误会打了起来，潘里斯伯爵被罗密欧杀死了。罗密欧发现自己杀死的是潘里斯伯爵，内心十分懊悔。他掘开了朱丽叶的坟墓，看着妻子的容颜，他喝下了毒药。

这时，劳伦思神父赶到了墓地，他发现自己来晚了，罗密欧已经服毒自杀了。过了不一会儿，朱丽叶就醒过来了，看着身边罗密欧的尸体，她一下子就明白了。随即朱丽叶用罗密欧的匕首自杀了。

墓地的骚乱把整个维罗纳城都吵醒了。亲王和两家的大人都赶到了墓地。听劳伦思神父原原本本地把事情的真相讲了出来，两家人都为两个年轻人感到惋惜，两家的仇恨在这一刻烟消云散。

人物事件词汇表

Capulet 开普莱特 朱丽叶家族的姓

Montague 蒙泰古 罗密欧家族的姓

Verona 维罗纳 意大利北部的一座历史悠久的城市

Romeo 罗密欧 老蒙泰古大人的儿子，故事的主人公

Benvolio 本沃利奥 罗密欧的好朋友

Mercutio 莫丘西奥 罗密欧的好朋友

Tybalt 提博尔特 老开普莱特大人的侄子

Juliet 朱丽叶 老开普莱特大人的女儿，故事的主人公

Lawrence 劳伦思 神父，罗密欧与朱丽叶爱情的见证者

Mantua 曼图阿 位于意大利北部，为文艺复兴时期重要的音乐中心，罗密欧的流放之地

Paris 潘里斯 朱丽叶的追求者

The two chief families in Verona were the rich Capulets and the Montagues. There had been an old quarrel between these families, which was grown to such a height, and so deadly was the enmity between them, that it extended to the remotest kindred, to the followers and retainers of both sides, insomuch that a servant of the house of Montague could not meet a servant of the house of Capulet, nor a Capulet encounter with a Montague by chance, but fierce words and sometimes bloodshed ensued; and frequent were the brawls from such accidental meetings, which disturbed the happy quiet of Verona's streets.

Old lord Capulet made a great supper, to which many fair ladies and many noble guests were invited. All the admired beauties of Verona were present, and all comers were made welcome if they were not of the house of Montague. At this feast of Capulets, Rosaline, beloved of Romeo, son to the old lord Montague, was present; and though it was dangerous for a Montague to be seen in this assembly, yet Benvolio, a friend of Romeo, persuaded the young lord to go to this assembly in the disguise of a mask, that he might see his Rosaline, and seeing her, compare her with some choice beauties of Verona, who (he said) would make him think his swan a crow. Romeo had small faith in Benvolio's words; nevertheless, for the love of Rosaline, he was persuaded to go. For Romeo was a sincere and passionate lover, and one that lost his sleep for love, and fled society to be alone, thinking on Rosaline, who disdained him, and never requited his love, with the least show of courtesy or affection; and Benvolio wished to cure his friend of this love by showing him diversity of ladies and company. To this feast of Capulets then young Romeo with Benvolio and their friend Mercutio went masked. Old Capulet bid them welcome, and told them that ladies who had their toes unplagued with corns would dance with them. And the old man was light hearted and merry, and said that he had worn a mask when he was young, and could have told a whispering tale in a fair lady's ear. And they fell to dancing, and Romeo was suddenly struck with the exceeding beauty of a lady who danced there, who seemed to him to teach the torches to burn bright, and her beauty to show by night like a rich jewel worn by a black-

罗密欧与朱丽叶

amoor; beauty too rich for use, too dear for earth! like a snowy dove trooping with crows (he said), so richly did her beauty and perfections shine above the ladies her companions. While he uttered these praises, he was overheard by Tybalt, a nephew of lord Capulet, who knew him by his voice to be Romeo. And this Tybalt, being of a fiery and passionate temper, could not endure that a Montague should come under cover of a mask, to fleer and scorn (as he said) at their solemnities. And he stormed and raged exceedingly, and would have struck young Romeo dead. But his uncle, the old lord Capulet, would not suffer him to do any injury at that time, both out of respect to his guests, and because Romeo had borne himself like a gentleman, and all tongues in Verona bragged of him to be a virtuous and well-governed youth. Tybalt, forced to be patient against his will, restrained himself, but swore that this vile Montague should at another time dearly pay for his intrusion.

The dancing being done, Romeo watched the place where the lady stood; and under favour of his masking habit, which might seem to excuse in part the liberty, he presumed in the gentlest manner to take her by the hand, calling it a shrine, which if he profaned by touching it, he was a blushing pilgrim, and would kiss it for atonement. 'Good pilgrim,' answered the lady, 'your devotion shows by far too mannerly and too courtly: saints have hands, which pilgrims may touch, but kiss not.' 'Have not saints lips, and pilgrims too?' said Romeo. 'Ay,' said the lady, 'lips which they must use in prayer.' 'O then, my dear saint,' said Romeo, 'hear my prayer, and grant it, lest I despair.' In such like allusions and loving conceits they were engaged, when the lady was called away to her mother. And Romeo inquiring who her mother was, discovered that the lady whose peerless beauty he was so much struck with, was young Juliet, daughter and heir to the lord Capulet, the great enemy of the Montagues; and that he had unknowingly engaged his heart to his foe. This troubled him, but it could not dissuade him from loving. As little rest had Juliet, when she found that the gentleman that she had been talking with was Romeo and a Montague, for she had been suddenly smit with the same hasty and inconsiderate passion for Romeo, which he had conceived for her; and a prodigious birth of love it seemed to her, that she must love her enemy, and that her afflictions should settle there, where family considerations should induce her chiefly to hate.

It being midnight, Romeo with his companions departed; but they soon missed him, for, unable to stay away from the house where he had left his heart, he leaped the wall of an orchard which was at the back of Juliet's house. Here he had not been long, ruminating on his new love, when Juliet appeared above at a window, through which her exceeding beauty seemed to break like the light of the sun in the east; and the moon, which shone in the orchard with a faint light, appeared to Romeo as if sick and pale with grief at the superior lustre of this new sun. And she, leaning her cheek upon her hand, he passionately wished himself a glove upon that hand, that he might touch her cheek. She all this while thinking herself alone, fetched a deep sigh, and exclaimed: 'Ah me!' Romeo, enraptured to hear her speak, said softly, and unheard by her: 'O speak again, bright angel, for such you appear, being over my head, like a winged messenger from heaven whom mortals fall back to gaze upon.' She, unconscious of being overheard, and full of the new passion which that night's adventure had given birth to, called upon her lover by name (whom she supposed absent): 'O Romeo, Romeo!' said she, 'wherefore art thou Romeo? Deny thy father, and refuse thy name, for my sake; or if thou wilt not, be but my sworn love, and I no longer will be a Capulet.'

Romeo, having this encouragement, would fain have spoken, but he was desirous of hearing more; and the lady continued her passionate discourse with herself (as she thought), still chiding Romeo for being Romeo and a Montague, and wishing him some other name, or that he would put away that hated name, and for that name which was no part of himself, he should take all herself. At this loving word Romeo could no longer refrain, but taking up the dialogue as if her words had been addressed to him personally, and not merely in fancy, he bade her call him Love, or by whatever other name she pleased, for he was no longer Romeo, if that name was displeasing to her. Juliet, alarmed to hear a man's voice in the garden, did not at first know who it was, that by favour of the night and darkness had thus stumbled upon the discovery of her secret; but when he spoke again, though her ears had not yet drunk a hundred words of that tongue's uttering, yet so nice is a lover's hearing, that she immediately knew him to be young Romeo, and she expostulated with him on the danger to which he had exposed himself by climbing the orchard walls, for if any of her kinsmen should find him there, it would be death to him, being a Montague. 'Alack,' said Romeo, 'there is more peril in your eye, than in twenty of their swords. Do you but look kind upon me, lady, and I am proof against their enmity. Better my life should be ended by their hate, than that hated life should be prolonged, to live without your love.' 'How came you into this place,' said Juliet, 'and by whose direction?' 'Love directed me,' answered Romeo: 'I am no pilot, yet wert thou as far apart from me, as that vast shore which is washed with the farthest sea, I should venture for such merchandise.' A crimson blush came over Juliet's face, yet unseen by Romeo by reason of the night, when she reflected upon the discovery which she had made, yet not meaning to make it, of her love to Romeo. She would fain have recalled her words, but that was impossible: fain would she have stood upon form, and have kept her lover at a distance, as the custom

美丽的朱丽叶

of discreet ladies is, to frown and be perverse, and give their suitors harsh denials at first; to stand off, and affect a coyness or indifference, where they most love, that their lovers may not think them too lightly or too easily won; for the difficulty of attainment increases the value of the object. But there was no room in her case for denials, or puttings off, or any of the customary arts of delay and protracted courtship. Romeo had heard from her own tongue, when she did not dream that he was near her, a confession of her love. So with an honest frankness, which the novelty of her situation excused, she confirmed the truth of what he had before heard, and addressing him by the name of fair Montague (love can sweeten a sour name), she begged him not to impute her easy yielding to levity or an unworthy mind, but that he must lay the fault of it (if it were a fault) upon the accident of the night which had so strangely discovered her thoughts. And she added, that though her behaviour to him might not be sufficiently prudent, measured by the custom of her sex, yet that she would prove more true than many whose prudence was dissembling, and their modesty artificial cunning.

Romeo was beginning to call the heavens to witness, that nothing was farther from his thoughts than to impute a shadow of dishonour to such an honoured lady, when she stopped him, begging him not to swear; for although she joyed in him, yet she had no joy of that night's contract: it was too rash, too unadvised, too sudden. But he being urgent with her to exchange a vow of love with him that night, she said that she already had given him hers before he requested it; meaning, when he overheard her confession; but she would retract what she then bestowed, for the pleasure of giving it again, for her bounty was as infinite as the sea, and her love as deep. From this loving conference she was called away by her nurse, who slept with her, and thought it time for her to be in bed, for it was near to daybreak; but hastily returning, she said three or four words more to Romeo, the purport of which was, that if his love was indeed honourable, and his purpose marriage, she would send a messenger to him to-morrow, to appoint a time for their marriage, when she would lay all her fortunes at his feet, and follow him as her lord through the world. While they were

朱丽叶的保姆

settling this point, Juliet was repeatedly called for by her nurse, and went in and returned, and went and returned again, for she seemed as jealous of Romeo going from her, as a young girl of her bird, which she will let hop a little from her hand, and pluck it back with a silken thread; and Romeo was as loath to part as she; for the sweetest music to lovers is the sound of each other's tongues at night. But at last they parted, wishing mutually sweet sleep and rest for that night.

The day was breaking when they parted, and Romeo, who was too full of thoughts of his mistress and that blessed meeting to allow him to sleep, instead of going home, bent his course to a monastery hard by, to find friar Lawrence. The good friar was already up at his devotions, but seeing young Romeo abroad so early, he conjectured rightly that he had not been abed that night, but that some distemper of youthful affection had kept him waking. He was right in imputing the cause of Romeo's wakefulness to love, but he made a wrong guess at the object, for he thought that his love for Rosaline had kept him waking. But when Romeo revealed his new passion for Juliet, and requested the assistance of the friar to marry them that day, the holy man lifted up his eyes and hands in a sort of wonder at the sudden change in Romeo's affections, for he had been privy to all Romeo's love for Rosaline, and his many complaints of her disdain: and he said, that young men's love lay not truly in their hearts, but in their eyes. But Romeo replying, that he himself had often chidden him for doting on Rosaline, who could not love him again, whereas Juliet both loved and was beloved by him, the friar assented in some measure to his reasons; and thinking that a matrimonial alliance between young Juliet and Romeo might happily be the means of making up the long breach between the Capulets and the Montagues; which no one more lamented than this good friar, who was a friend to both the families and had often interposed his mediation to make up the quarrel without effect; partly moved by policy, and partly by his fondness for young Romeo, to whom he could deny nothing, the old man consented to join their hands in marriage.

劳伦思神父

Now was Romeo blessed indeed, and Juliet, who knew his intent from a messenger which she had despatched according to promise, did not fail to be early at the cell of friar Lawrence, where their hands were joined in holy marriage; the good friar praying the heavens to smile upon that act, and in the union of this young Montague and young Capulet to bury the old strife and long dissensions of their families.

The ceremony being over, Juliet hastened home, where she stayed impatient for the coming of night, at which time Romeo promised to come and meet her in the orchard, where they had met the night before; and the time between seemed as tedious to her, as the night before some great festival seems to an impatient child, that has got new finery which it may not put on till the morning.

That same day, about noon, Romeo's friends, Benvolio and Mercutio, walking through the streets of Verona, were met by a party of the Capulets with the impetuous Tybalt at their head. This was the same angry Tybalt who would have fought with Romeo at old lord Capulet's feast. He, seeing Mercutio, accused him bluntly of associating with Romeo, a Montague. Mercutio, who had as much fire and youthful blood in him as Tybalt, replied to this accusation with some sharpness; and in spite of all Benvolio could say to moderate their wrath, a quarrel was beginning, when Romeo himself passing that way, the fierce Tybalt turned from Mercutio to Romeo, and gave him the disgraceful appellation of villain. Romeo wished to avoid a quarrel with Tybalt above all men, because he was the kinsman of Juliet, and much beloved by her; besides, this young Montague had never thoroughly entered into the family quarrel, being by nature wise and gentle, and the name of a Capulet, which was his dear lady's name, was now rather a charm to allay resentment, than a watchword to excite fury. So he tried to reason with Tybalt, whom he saluted mildly by the name of good Capulet, as if he, though a Montague, had some secret pleasure in uttering that name: but Tybalt, who hated all Montagues as he hated hell, would hear no reason, but drew his weapon; and Mercutio, who knew not of Romeo's secret motive for desiring peace with Tybalt, but looked upon his present forbearance as a sort of calm dishonourable submission, with many disdainful words provoked Tybalt to the prosecution of his first quarrel with him; and Tybalt and Mercutio fought, till Mercutio fell, receiving his death's wound while Romeo and Benvolio were vainly endeavouring to part the combatants. Mercutio being dead, Romeo kept his temper no longer, but returned the scornful appellation of villain which Tybalt had given him; and they fought till Tybalt was slain by Romeo. This deadly broil falling out in the midst of Verona at noonday, the news of it quickly brought a crowd of citizens to the spot, and among them the old lords Capulet and Montague, with their wives; and soon after arrived the prince himself, who being related to Mercutio, whom Tybalt had slain, and having had the peace of his government often disturbed by these brawls of Montagues and Capulets, came determined to put the law in strictest force against those who should be found to be offenders. Benvolio, who had been eyewitness to the fray, was commanded by the prince to relate the origin of it, which he did, keeping as near the truth as he could without injury to Romeo, softening and excusing the part which his friends took in it. Lady Capulet, whose extreme grief for the loss of her kinsman Tybalt made her keep no bounds in her revenge, exhorted the prince to do strict justice upon his murderer, and to pay no attention to Benvolio's representation, who, being Romeo's friend and a Montague, spoke partially. Thus she pleaded against her new son-in-law, but she knew not yet that he was her son-in-law and Juliet's husband. On the other hand was to be seen Lady Montague pleading for her child's life, and arguing with some justice that Romeo had done nothing worthy of punishment in taking the life of Tybalt, which was already forfeited to the law by his having slain Mercutio. The prince, unmoved by the passionate exclamations of these women, on a careful examination of the facts, pronounced his sentence, and by that sentence Romeo was banished from Verona.

Heavy news to young Juliet, who had been but a few hours a bride, and now by this decree seemed everlastingly divorced! When the tidings reached her, she at first gave way to rage against Romeo, who had slain her dear cousin: she called him a beautiful tyrant, a fiend angelical, a ravenous dove, a lamb with a wolf's nature, a serpent-heart hid with a flowering face, and other like contradictory names, which denoted the struggles in her mind between her love and her resentment: but in the end love got the mastery, and the tears which she shed for grief that Romeo had slain her cousin, turned to drops of joy that her husband lived whom Tybalt would have slain. Then came fresh tears, and they were altogether of grief for Romeo's banishment. That word was more terrible to her than the death of many Tybalts.

Romeo, after the fray, had taken refuge in friar Lawrence's cell, where he was first made acquainted with the prince's sentence, which seemed to him far more terrible than death. To him it appeared there was no world out of Verona's walls, no living out of the sight of Juliet. Heaven was there where Juliet lived, and all beyond was purgatory, torture, hell. The good friar would have applied the consolation of philosophy to his griefs: but this frantic young man would hear of none, but like a madman he tore his hair, and threw himself all along upon the ground, as he said, to take the measure of his grave. From this

罗密欧悲恸万分

unseemly state he was roused by a message from his dear lady, which a little revived him; and then the friar took the advantage to expostulate with him on the unmanly weakness which he had shown. He had slain Tybalt, but would he also slay himself, slay his dear lady, who lived but in his life? The noble form of man, he said, was but a shape of wax, when it wanted the courage which should keep it firm. The law had been lenient to him, that instead of death, which he had incurred, had pronounced by the prince's mouth only banishment. He had slain Tybalt, but Tybalt would have slain him: there was a sort of happiness in that. Juliet was alive, and (beyond all hope) had become his dear wife; therein he was most happy. All these blessings, as the friar made them out to be, did Romeo put from him like a sullen misbehaved wench. And the friar bade him beware, for such as despaired, (he said) died miserable. Then when Romeo was a little calmed, he counselled him that he should go that night and secretly take his leave of Juliet, and thence proceed straightways to Mantua, at which place he should sojourn, till the friar found fit occasion to publish his marriage, which might be a joyful means of reconciling their families; and then he did not doubt but the prince would be moved to pardon him, and he would return with twenty times more joy than he went forth with grief. Romeo was convinced by these wise counsels of the friar, and took his leave to go and seek his lady, proposing to stay with her that night, and by daybreak pursue his journey alone to Mantua; to which place the good friar promised to send him letters from time to time, acquainting him with the state of affairs at home.

That night Romeo passed with his dear wife, gaining secret admission to her chamber, from the orchard in which he had heard her confession of love the night before. That had been a night of unmixed joy and rapture; but the pleasures of this night, and the delight which these lovers took in each other's society, were sadly allayed with the prospect of parting, and the fatal adventures of the past day. The unwelcome daybreak seemed to come too soon, and when Juliet heard the morning song of the lark, she would have persuaded herself that it was the nightingale, which sings by night, but it was too truly the lark which sang, and a discordant and unpleasing note it seemed to her; and the streaks of day in the east too certainly pointed out that it was time for these lovers to part. Romeo took his leave of his dear wife with a heavy heart, promising to write to her from Mantua every hour in the day; and when he had descended from her chamber-window, as he stood below her on the ground, in that sad foreboding state of mind in which she was, he appeared to her eyes as one dead in the bottom of a tomb. Romeo's mind misgave him in like manner: but now he was forced hastily to depart, for it was death for him to be found within the walls of Verona after daybreak.

This was but the beginning of the tragedy of this pair of star-crossed lovers. Romeo had not been gone many days, before the old lord Capulet proposed a match for Juliet. The husband he had chosen for her, not dreaming that she was married already, was count Paris, a gallant, young, and noble gentleman, no unworthy suitor to the young Juliet, if she had never seen Romeo.

The terrified Juliet was in a sad perplexity at her father's offer. She pleaded her youth unsuitable to marriage, the recent death of Tybalt, which had left her spirits too weak to meet a husband with any face of joy, and how indecorous it would show for the family of the Capulets to be celebrating a nuptial feast, when his funeral solemnities were hardly over: she pleaded every reason against the match, but the true one, namely, that she was married already. But lord Capulet was deaf to all her excuses, and in a peremptory manner ordered her to get ready, for by the following Thursday she should be married to Paris: and having found her a husband, rich, young, and noble, such as the proudest maid in Verona might joyfully accept, he could not bear that out of an affected coyness, as he construed her denial, she should oppose obstacles to her own good fortune.

In this extremity Juliet applied to the friendly friar, always her counsellor in distress, and he asking her if she had resolution to undertake a desperate remedy, and she answering that she would go into the grave alive rather than marry Paris, her own dear husband living; he directed her to go home, and appear merry, and give her consent to marry Paris, according to her father's desire, and on the next night, which was the night before the marriage, to drink off the contents of a phial which he then gave her, the effect of which would be that for two-and-forty hours after drinking it she should appear cold and lifeless; and when the bridegroom came to fetch her in the morning, he would find her to appearance dead; that then she would be borne, as the manner in that country was, uncovered on a bier, to be buried in the family vault; that if she could put off womanish fear, and consent to this terrible trial, in forty-two hours after swallowing the liquid (such was its certain operation) she would be sure to awake, as from a dream; and before she should awake, he would let her husband know their drift, and he should come in the night, and bear her thence to Mantua. Love, and the dread of marrying Paris, gave young Juliet strength to undertake this horrible adventure; and she took the phial of the friar, promising to observe his directions.

Going from the monastery, she met the young count Paris, and modestly dissembling, promised to become his bride. This was joyful news to the lord Capulet and his wife. It seemed to put youth into the old man; and Juliet, who had displeased him exceedingly, by her refusal of the count, was his darling again, now she promised to be obedient. All things in the house were in a bustle against the approaching nuptials. No cost was spared to prepare such festival rejoicings as Verona had never before witnessed.

On the Wednesday night Juliet drank off the potion. She had many misgivings lest the friar, to avoid the blame which might be imputed to him for marrying her to Romeo, had given her poison; but then he was always known for a holy man: then lest she should awake before the time that Romeo was to come for her; whether the terror of the place, a vault of dead Capulets' bones, and where Tybalt, all bloody, lay festering in his shroud, would not be enough to drive her distracted: again she thought of all the stories she had heard of spirits haunting the places where their bodies were bestowed. But then her love for Romeo, and her aversion for Paris returned, and she desperately swallowed the draught and became insensible.

When young Paris came early in the morning with music to awaken his bride, instead of a living Juliet, her chamber presented the dreary spectacle of a lifeless corset. What death to his hopes! What confusion then reigned through the whole house! Poor Paris lamenting his bride, whom most detestable death had beguiled him of, had divorced from him even before their hands were joined. But still more piteous it was to hear the mournings of the old lord and lady Capulet, who having but this one, one poor loving child to rejoice and solace in, cruel death had snatched her from their sight, just as these careful parents were on the point of seeing her advanced (as they thought) by a promising and advantageous match. Now all things that were ordained for the festival were turned from their properties to do the office of a black funeral. The wedding cheer served for a sad burial feast, the bridal hymns were changed for sullen dirges, the sprightly instruments to melancholy bells, and the flowers that should have been strewed in the bride's path, now served but to strew her corset. Now, instead of a priest to marry her, a priest was needed to bury her; and she was borne to church indeed, not to augment the cheerful hopes of the living, but to swell the dreary numbers of the dead.

Bad news, which always travels faster than good, now brought the dismal story of his Juliet's death to Romeo, at Mantua, before the messenger could arrive, who was sent from friar Lawrence to apprise him that these were mock funerals only, and but the shadow and representation of death, and that his dear lady lay in the tomb but for a short while, expecting when Romeo would come to release her from that dreary mansion. Just before, Romeo had been unusually joyful and light-hearted. He had dreamed in the night that he was dead (a strange dream, that gave a dead man leave to think), and that his lady came and found him dead, and breathed such life with kisses in his lips, that he revived, and was an emperor! And now that a messenger came from Verona, he thought surely it was to confirm some good news which his dreams had presaged. But when the contrary to this flattering vision appeared, and that it was his lady who was dead in truth, whom he could not revive by any kisses, he ordered horses to be got ready, for he determined that night to visit Verona, and to see his lady in her tomb. And as mischief is swift to enter into the thoughts of desperate men, he called to mind a poor apothecary, whose shop in Mantua he had lately passed, and from the beggarly appearance of the man, who seemed famished, and the wretched show in his show of empty boxes ranged on dirty shelves, and other tokens of extreme wretchedness, he had said at the time (perhaps having some misgivings that his own disastrous life might haply meet with a conclusion so desperate), 'If a man were to need poison, which by the law of Mantua it is death to sell, here lives a poor wretch who would sell it him.' These words of his now came into his mind, and he sought out the apothecary, who after some pretended scruples, Romeo offering him gold, which his poverty could not resist, sold him a poison, which, if he swallowed, he told him, if he had the strength of twenty men, would quickly despatch him.

With this poison he set out for Verona, to have a sight of his dear lady in her tomb, meaning, when he had satisfied his sight, to swallow the poison, and be buried by her side. He reached Verona at midnight, and found the churchyard, in the midst of which was situated the ancient tomb of the Capulets. He had provided a light, and a spade, and wrenching iron, and was proceeding to break open the monument, when he was interrupted by a voice, which by the name of vile Montague, bade him desist from his unlawful business. It was the young count Paris, who had come to the tomb of Juliet at that unseasonable time of night, to strew flowers and to weep over the grave of her that should have been his bride. He knew not what an interest Romeo had in the dead, but knowing him to be a Montague, and (as he supposed) a sworn foe to all the Capulets, he judged that he was come by night to do some villanous shame to the dead bodies; therefore in an angry tone he bade him desist; and as a criminal, condemned by the laws of Verona to die if he were found within the walls of the city, he would have apprehended him. Romeo urged Paris to leave him, and warned him by the fate of Tybalt, who lay buried there, not to provoke his anger, or draw down another sin upon his head, by forcing him to kill him. But the count in scorn refused his warning, and laid hands on him as a felon, which Romeo resisting, they fought, and Paris fell. When Romeo, by the help of a light, came to see who it was that he had slain, that it was Paris, who (he learned in his way from Mantua) should have married Juliet, he took the dead youth by the hand, as one whom misfortune had made a companion, and said that he would bury him in a triumphal grave, meaning in Juliet's grave, which he now opened: and

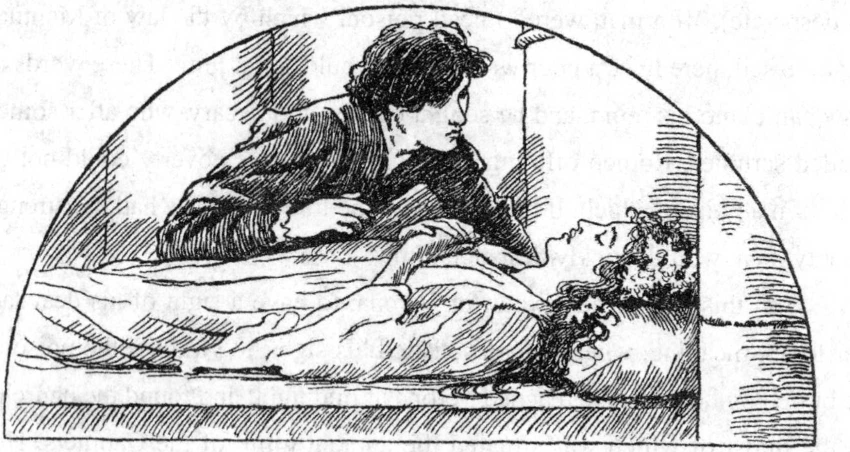

看到了心爱的人

there lay his lady, as one whom death had no power upon to change a feature or complexion, in her matchless beauty; or as if Death were amorous, and the lean abhorred monster kept her there for his delight; for she lay yet fresh and blooming, as she had fallen to sleep when she swallowed that benumbing potion; and near her lay Tybalt in his bloody shroud, whom Romeo seeing, begged pardon of his lifeless corse, and for Juliet's sake called him cousin, and said that he was about to do him a favour by putting his enemy to death. Here Romeo took his last leave of his lady's lips, kissing them; and here he shook the burden of his cross stars from his weary body, swallowing that poison which the apothecary had sold him, whose operation was fatal and real, not like that dissembling potion which Juliet had swallowed, the effect of which was now nearly expiring, and she about to awake to complain that Romeo had not kept his time, or that he had come too soon.

For now the hour was arrived at which the friar had promised that she should awake; and he, having learned that his letters which he had sent to Mantua, by some unlucky detention of the messenger, had never reached Romeo, came himself, provided with the pickaxe and lantern, to deliver the lady from her confinement; but he was surprised to find a light already burning in the Capulets' monument, and to see swords and blood near it, and Romeo and Paris lying breathless by the monument.

Before he could entertain a conjecture, to imagine how these fatal accidents had fallen out, Juliet awoke out of her trance, and seeing the friar near her, she remembered the place where she was, and the occasion of her being there, and asked for Romeo, but the friar, hearing a noise, bade her come out of that place of death, and of unnatural sleep, for a greater power than they could contradict had thwarted their intents; and being frightened by the noise of people coming, he fled: but when Juliet saw the cup closed in her true love's hand, she guessed that poison had been the cause of his end, and she would have swallowed the dregs if any had been left, and she kissed his still warm lips to try if any poison yet did hang upon them, then hearing a nearer noise of people coming, she quickly unsheathed a dagger which she wore, and stabbing herself, died by her true Romeo's side.

The watch by this time had come up to the place. A page belonging to count Paris, who had witnessed the fight between his master and Romeo, had given the alarm, which had spread among the citizens, who went up and down the streets of Verona confusedly exclaiming, A Paris! a Romeo! a Juliet! as the rumour had imperfectly reached them, till the uproar brought lord Montague and lord Capulet out of their beds, with the prince, to inquire into the causes of the disturbance. The friar had been apprehended by some of the watch, coming from the churchyard, trembling, sighing, and weeping, in a suspicious manner. A great multitude being assembled at the Capulets' monument, the friar was demanded by the prince to deliver what he knew of these strange and disastrous accidents.

And there, in the presence of the old lords Montague and Capulet, he faithfully related the story of their children's fatal love, the part he took in promoting their marriage, in the hope in that union to end the long quarrels between their families: how Romeo, there dead, was husband to Juliet; and Juliet, there dead, was Romeo's faithful wife; how before he could find a fit opportunity to divulge their marriage, another match was projected for Juliet, who, to avoid the crime of a second marriage, swallowed the sleeping draught (as he advised), and all thought her dead; how meantime he wrote to Romeo, to come and take her thence when the force of the potion should cease, and by what unfortunate miscarriage of the messenger the letters never reached Romeo: further than this the friar could not follow the story, nor knew more than that coming himself, to deliver Juliet from that place of death, he found the count Paris and Romeo slain. The remainder of the transactions was supplied by the narration of the page who had seen Paris and Romeo fight, and by the servant who came with Romeo from Verona, to whom this faithful lover had given letters to be delivered to his father in the event of his death, which made good the friar's words, confessing his marriage with Juliet, imploring the forgiveness of his parents, acknowledging the buying of the poison of the poor apothecary, and his intent in coming to the monument, to die, and lie with Juliet. All these circumstances agreed together to clear the friar from any hand he could be supposed to have in these complicated slaughters, further than as the unintended consequences of his own well meant, yet too artificial and subtle contrivances.

And the prince, turning to these old lords, Montague and Capulet, rebuked them for their brutal and irrational enmities, and showed them what a scourge Heaven had laid upon such offences, that it had found means even through the love of their children to punish their unnatural hate. And these old rivals, no longer enemies, agreed to bury their long strife in their children's graves; and lord Capulet requested lord Montague to give him his hand, calling him by the name of brother, as if in acknowledgment of the union of their families, by the marriage of the young Capulet and Montague; and saying that lord Montague's hand (in token of reconcilement) was all he demanded for his daughter's jointure: but lord Montague said he would give him more, for he would raise her a statue of pure gold, that while Verona kept its name, no figure should be so esteemed for its richness and workmanship as that of the true and faithful Juliet. And lord Capulet in return said that he would raise another statue to Romeo. So did these poor old lords, when it was too late, strive to outgo each other in mutual courtesies: while so deadly had been their rage and enmity in past times, that nothing but the fearful overthrow of their children (poor sacrifices to their quarrels and dissensions) could remove the rooted hates and jealousies of the noble families.

哈姆雷特

Hamlet

导读

丹麦王后戈楚德在国王去世不到两个月就要下嫁给国王的弟弟克劳迪斯了。许多人都怀疑是克劳迪斯害死了国王，从而取而代之。母亲这个轻率的举动深深伤害了王子哈姆雷特，他对整个世界都感到绝望，做什么事情都打不起精神。无论母亲和叔叔如何劝慰他，他都高兴不起来，也拒绝参加一切社交活动。

他怀疑是叔叔害死了父亲，而对于母亲在这场阴谋中究竟扮演着什么角色，他又完全不敢去猜测，这让他更加苦恼。

宫中传说有一个鬼魂出现在城堡，卫兵们觉得鬼魂长得像死去的国王。哈姆雷特认定这是父亲有话要说。于是他带着自己的朋友一起去等待鬼魂的出现。看到鬼魂，哈姆雷特立刻就认出了，那正是自己父亲的鬼魂。鬼魂要和哈姆雷特单独交谈，哈姆雷特答应了。鬼魂告诉哈姆雷特，他是被自己的弟弟害死的，而弟弟的目的就是霸占他的妻子和王位，他请哈姆雷特为自己报仇。但在报仇的时候千万不要伤害到王后，也就是哈姆雷特的母亲。哈姆雷特答应了鬼魂的要求，鬼魂立刻消失了。这天晚上发生的事，哈姆雷特只告诉了霍拉提奥一个人，并且他要霍拉提奥严守这个秘密。

哈姆雷特担心自己的行为会被叔叔看出端倪，于是决定开始装疯。甚至在他所钟爱的女子面前，他也和一个疯子没有两样。但是他偶尔表露出的温情让他的母亲和叔叔以为他发疯是因为爱情。

但是哈姆雷特明白自己装疯的真正原因。他无时无刻不想杀死叔叔，但是叔叔身边总是有很多的卫士，同时王后又总是陪在他身边。有时哈姆雷特又怀疑自己是受了魔鬼的诱惑，这一切都不是真的。

认出那是父亲的鬼魂

这天，有一个戏班演出了一场戏剧，内容正是一个受人爱戴的国王被谋害的故事。哈姆雷特被这出戏深深打动了。他想出了个主意，让戏班演戏给国王看，到时候看国王有什么表现，这样就能知道是不是他谋害了老国王。

国王和王后发现剧中的表演和自己的行为如此的相似，都感到恐惧。国王早早就离开了座位。这让哈姆雷特确定，就是他们谋害了自己的父亲。

演出结束后，王后受国王的指派把哈姆雷特叫去说教了一番，同时国王还安排大臣偷听了母子的谈话。

哈姆雷特斥责自己的母亲堕落，竟然背叛自己的丈夫。这让王后感到羞愧万分。哈姆雷特要求母亲坚守本分，王后答应了。

国王找借口把哈姆雷特遣送去英国，同时写信要求英国人帮忙杀死哈姆雷特。机智的哈姆雷特在一次海盗冲突中巧妙地逃脱了。

后来哈姆雷特悄悄地回到了丹麦。在那里他发现自己所钟爱的姑娘已经死去，他更加悲痛。那姑娘的哥哥受到国王的怂恿，要与哈姆雷特进行一场决斗。国王在姑娘哥哥的剑上涂上了毒药，想要趁机杀死哈姆雷特。在比试过程中，哈姆雷特被刺伤了，而哈姆雷特夺过剑把对手也刺伤了。两个年轻人都要死了。这时，王后因为误喝了国王为哈姆雷特准备的毒药被毒死了。哈姆雷特用尽最后的力量把剑刺进了国王的胸膛。最终，哈姆雷特在死前实现了为父亲报仇的承诺。

人物事件词汇表

Denmark　丹麦 斯堪的纳维亚组成国家之一

Gertrude　戈楚德 丹麦王后，哈姆雷特的母亲

Claudius　克劳迪斯 已故国王的弟弟

Hamlet　哈姆雷特 丹麦王子，已故国王的儿子，故事的主人公

Horatio　霍拉提奥 哈姆雷特的好友

Gertrude, queen of Denmark, becoming a widow by the sudden death of King Hamlet, in less than two months after his death married his brother Claudius, which was noted by all people at the time for a strange act of indiscretion, or unfeelingness, or worse: for this Claudius did no ways resemble her late husband in the qualities of his person or his mind, but was as contemptible in outward appearance, as he was base and unworthy in disposition; and suspicions did not fail to arise in the minds of some, that he had privately made away with his brother, the late king, with the view of marrying his widow, and ascending the throne of Denmark, to the exclusion of young Hamlet, the son of the buried king, and lawful successor to the throne.

But upon no one did this unadvised action of the queen make such impression as upon this young prince, who loved and venerated the memory of his dead father almost to idolatry, and being of a nice sense of honour, and a most exquisite practicer of propriety himself, did sorely take to heart this unworthy conduct of his mother Gertrude: insomuch that, between grief for his father's death and shame for his mother's marriage, this young prince was overclouded with a deep melancholy, and lost all his mirth and all his good looks; all his customary pleasure in books forsook him, his princely exercises and sports, proper to his youth, were no longer acceptable; he grew weary of the world, which seemed to him an unweeded garden, where all the wholesome flowers were choked up, and nothing but weeds could thrive. Not that the prospect of exclusion from the throne, his lawful inheritance, weighed so much upon his spirits, though that to a young and high-minded prince was a bitter wound and a sore indignity; but what so galled him, and took away all his cheerful spirits, was, that his mother had shown herself so forgetful to his father's memory; and such a father! who had been to her so loving and so gentle a husband! and then she always appeared as loving and obedient a wife to him, and would hang upon him as if her affection grew to him: and now within two months, or as it seemed to young Hamlet, less than two months, she had married again, married his uncle, her dear husband's brother, in itself a highly improper and unlawful marriage, from the nearness of relationship, but made much more so by the indecent haste with which it was concluded, and the unkingly character of the man whom she had chosen to be the partner of her throne and bed. This it was, which more than the loss of ten kingdoms, dashed the spirits and brought a cloud over the mind of this honourable young prince.

In vain was all that his mother Gertrude or the king could do to contrive to divert him; he still appeared in court in a suit of deep black, as mourning for the king his father's death, which mode of dress he had never laid aside, not even in compliment to his mother upon the day she was married, nor could he be brought to join in any of the festivities or rejoicings of that (as appeared to him) disgraceful day.

What mostly troubled him was an uncertainty about the manner of his father's death. It was given out by Claudius that a serpent had stung him; but young Hamlet had shrewd suspicions that Claudius himself was the serpent; in plain English, that he had murdered him for his crown, and that the serpent who stung his father did now sit on the throne.

How far he was right in this conjecture, and what he ought to think of his mother, how far she was privy to this murder, and whether by her consent or knowledge, or without, it came to pass, were the doubts which continually harassed and distracted him.

A rumour had reached the ear of young Hamlet, that an apparition, exactly resembling the dead king his father, had been seen by the soldiers upon watch, on the platform before the palace at midnight, for two or three nights successively. The figure came constantly clad in the same suit of armour, from head to foot, which the dead king was known to have worn: and they who saw it (Hamlet's bosom friend Horatio was one) agreed in their testimony as to the time and manner of its appearance: that it came just as the clock struck twelve; that it looked pale, with a face more of sorrow than of anger; that its beard was grisly, and the colour a sable silvered, as they had seen it in his lifetime: that it made no answer when they spoke to it; yet once they thought it lifted up its head, and addressed itself to motion, as if it were about to speak; but in that moment the morning cock crew, and it shrunk in haste away, and vanished out of their sight.

The young prince, strangely amazed at their relation, which was too consistent and agreeing with itself to disbelieve, concluded that it was his father's ghost which they had seen, and determined to take his watch with the soldiers that night, that he might have a chance of seeing it; for he reasoned with himself, that such an appearance did not come for nothing, but that the ghost had something to impart, and though it had been silent hitherto, yet it would speak to him. And he waited with impatience for the coming of night.

国王与王后

When night came he took his stand with Horatio, and Marcellus, one of the guard, upon the platform, where this apparition was accustomed to walk: and it being a cold night, and the air unusually raw and nipping, Hamlet and Horatio and their companion fell into some talk about the coldness of the night, which was suddenly broken off by Horatio announcing that the ghost was coming.

At the sight of his father's spirit, Hamlet was struck with a sudden surprise and fear. He at first called upon the angels and heavenly ministers to defend them, for he knew not whether it were a good spirit or bad; whether it came for good or evil: but he gradually assumed more courage; and his father (as it seemed to him) looked upon him so piteously, and as it were desiring to have conversation with him, and did in all respects appear so like himself as he was when he lived, that Hamlet could not help addressing him: he called him by his name, Hamlet, King, Father! and conjured him that he would tell the reason why he had left his grave, where they had seen him quietly bestowed, to come again and visit the earth and the moonlight: and besought him that he would let them know if there was anything which they could do to give peace to his spirit. And the ghost beckoned to Hamlet, that he should go with him to some more removed place, where they might be alone; and Horatio and Marcellus would have dissuaded the young prince from following it, for they feared lest it should be some evil spirit, who would tempt him to the neighbouring sea, or to the top of some dreadful cliff, and there put on some horrible shape which might deprive the prince of his reason. But their counsels and entreaties could not alter Hamlet's determination, who cared too little about life to fear the losing of it; and as to his soul, he said, what could the spirit do to that, being a thing immortal as itself? And he felt as hardy as a lion, and bursting from them, who did all they could to hold him, he followed whithersoever the spirit led him.

And when they were alone together, the spirit broke silence, and told him that he was the ghost of Hamlet, his father, who had been cruelly murdered, and he told the manner of it; that it was done by his own brother Claudius, Hamlet's uncle, as Hamlet had already but too much suspected, for the hope of succeeding to his bed and crown. That as he was sleeping in his garden, his custom always in the afternoon, his treasonous brother stole upon him in his sleep, and poured the juice of poisonous henbane into his ears, which has such an antipathy to the life of man, that swift as quicksilver it courses through all the veins of the body, baking up the blood, and spreading a crustlike leprosy all over the skin: thus sleeping, by a brother's hand he was cut off at once from his crown, his queen, and his life: and he adjured Hamlet, if he did ever his dear father love that he would revenge his foul murder. And the ghost lamented to his son, that his mother should so fall off from virtue, as to prove false to the wedded love of her first husband, and to marry his murderer, but he cautioned Hamlet, howsoever he proceeded in his revenge against his wicked uncle, by no means to act

老国王的鬼魂

any violence against the person of his mother, but to leave her to heaven, and to the stings and thorns of conscience. And Hamlet promised to observe the ghost's direction in all things, and the ghost vanished.

And when Hamlet was left alone, he took up a solemn resolution, that all he had in his memory, all that he had ever learned by books or observation, should be instantly forgotten by him, and nothing live in his brain but the memory of what the ghost had told him, and enjoined him to do. And Hamlet related the particulars of the conversation which had passed to none but his dear friend Horatio; and he enjoined both to him and Marcellus the strictest secrecy as to what they had seen that night.

The terror which the sight of the ghost had left upon the senses of Hamlet, he being weak and dispirited before, almost unhinged his mind, and drove him beside his reason. And he, fearing that it would continue to have this effect, which might subject him to observation, and set his uncle upon his guard, if he suspected that he was meditating anything against him, or that Hamlet really knew more of his father's death than he professed, took up a strange resolution, from that time to counterfeit as if he were really and truly mad; thinking that he would be less an object of suspicion when his uncle should believe him incapable of any serious project, and that his real perturbation of mind would be best covered and pass concealed under a disguise of pretended lunacy.

From this time Hamlet affected a certain wildness and strangeness in his apparel, his speech, and behaviour, and did so excellently conterfeit the madman, that the king and queen were both deceived, and not thinking his grief for his father's death a sufficient cause to produce such a distemper, for they knew not of the appearance of the ghost, they concluded that his malady was love, and they thought they had found out the object.

Before Hamlet fell into the melancholy way which has been related, he had dearly loved a fair maid called Ophelia, the daughter of Polonius, the king's chief counsellor in affairs of state. He had sent her letters and rings, and made many tenders of his affection to her, and importuned her with love in honourable fashion: and she had given belief to his vows and importunities. But the melancholy which he fell into latterly had made him neglect her, and from the time he conceived the project of counterfeiting madness, he affected to treat her with unkindness, and a sort of rudeness: but she good lady, rather than reproach him with being false to her, persuaded herself that it was nothing but the disease in his mind, and no settled unkindness, which had made him less observant of her than formerly; and she compared the faculties of his once noble mind and excellent understanding, impaired as they were with the deep melancholy that oppressed him, to sweet bells which in themselves are capable of most exquisite music, but when jangled out of tune, or rudely handled, produce only a harsh and unpleasing sound.

心爱的姑娘

Though the rough business which Hamlet had in hand, the revenging of his father's death upon his murderer, did not suit with the playful state of courtship, or admit of the society of so idle a passion as love now seemed to him, yet it could not hinder but that soft thoughts of his Ophelia would come between, and in one of these moments, when he thought that his treatment of this gentle lady had been unreasonably harsh, he wrote her a letter full of wild starts of passion, and in extravagant terms, such as agreed with his supposed madness, but mixed with some gentle touches of affection, which could not but show to this honoured lady that a deep love for her yet lay at the bottom of his heart. He bade her to doubt the stars were fire, and to doubt that the sun did move, to doubt truth to be a liar, but never to doubt that he loved; with more of such extravagant phrases. This letter Ophelia dutifully showed to her father, and the old man thought himself bound to communicate it to the king and queen, who from that time supposed that the true cause of Hamlet's madness was love. And the queen wished that the good beauties of Ophelia might be the happy cause of his wildness, for so she hoped that her virtues might happily restore him to his accustomed way again, to both their honours.

But Hamlet's malady lay deeper than she supposed, or than could be so cured. His father's ghost, which he had seen, still haunted his imagination, and the sacred injunction to revenge his murder gave him no rest till it was accomplished. Every hour of delay seemed to him a sin, and a violation of his father's commands. Yet how to compass the death of the king, surrounded as he constantly was with his guards, was no easy matter. Or if it had been, the presence of the queen, Hamlet's mother, who was generally with the king, was a restraint upon his purpose, which he could not break through. Besides, the very circumstance that the usurper was his mother's husband filled him with some remorse, and still blunted the edge of his purpose. The mere act of putting a fellow-creature to death was in itself odious and terrible to a disposition naturally so gentle as Hamlet's was. His very melancholy, and the dejection of spirits he had so long been in, produced an irresoluteness and wavering of purpose which kept him from proceeding to extremities. Moreover, he could not help having some scruples upon his mind, whether the spirit which he had seen was indeed his father, or whether it might not be the devil, who he had heard has power to take any form he pleases, and who might have assumed his father's shape only to take advantage of his weakness and his melancholy, to drive him to the doing of so desperate an act as murder. And he determined that he would have more certain grounds to go upon than a vision, or apparition, which might be a delusion.

While he was in this irresolute mind there came to the court certain players, in whom Hamlet formerly used to take delight, and particularly to hear one of them speak a tragical speech, describing the death of old Priam, King of Troy, with the grief of Hecuba his queen. Hamlet welcomed his old friends, the players, and remembering how that speech had formerly given him pleasure, requested the player to repeat it; which he did in so lively a manner, setting forth the cruel murder of the feeble old king, with the destruction of his people and city by fire, and the mad grief of the old queen, running barefoot up and down the palace, with a poor clout upon that head where a crown had been, and with nothing but a blanket upon her loins, snatched up in haste, where she had worn a royal robe; that not only it drew tears from all that stood by, who thought they saw the real scene, so lively was it represented, but even the player himself delivered it with a broken voice and real tears. This put Hamlet upon thinking, if that player could so work himself up to passion by a mere fictitious speech, to weep for one that he had never seen, for Hecuba, that had been dead so many hundred years, how dull was he, who having a read motive and cue for passion, a real king and a dear father murdered, was yet so little moved, that his revenge all this while had seemed to have slept in dull and muddy forgetfulness! and while he meditated on actors and acting, and the powerful effects which a good play, represented to the life, has upon the spectator, he remembered the instance of some murderer, who seeing a murder on the stage, was by the mere force of the scene and resemblance of circumstances so affected, that on the spot he confessed the crime which he had committed. And he determined that these players should play something like the murder of his father before his uncle, and he would watch narrowly what effect it might have upon him, and from his looks he would be able to gather with more certainty if he were the murderer or not. To this effect he ordered a play to be prepared, to the representation of which he invited the king and queen.

The story of the play was of a murder done in Vienna upon a duke. The duke's name was Gonzago, his wife Baptista. The play showed how one Lucianus, a near relation to the duke, poisoned him in his garden for his estate, and how the murderer in a short time after got the love of Gonzago's wife.

At the representation of this play, the king, who did not know the trap which was laid for him, was present, with his queen and the whole court: Hamlet sitting attentively near him to observe his looks. The play began with a conversation between Gonzago and his wife, in which the lady made many protestations of love, and of never marrying a second husband, if she should outlive Gonzago; wishing she might be accursed if she ever took a second husband, and adding that no woman did so, but those wicked women who kill their first husbands. Hamlet observed the king his uncle change colour at this expression, and that it was as bad as wormwood both to him and to the queen. But when Lucianus, according to the story, came to poison Gonzago sleeping in the garden, the strong resemblance which it bore to his own wicked act upon the late king, his brother, whom he had poisoned in his garden, so struck upon the conscience of this usurper, that he was unable to sit out the rest of the play, but on a sudden calling for lights to his chamber, and affecting or partly feeling a sudden sickness, he abruptly left the theatre. The king being departed, the play was given over. Now Hamlet had seen enough to be satisfied that the words of the ghost were true, and no illusion; and in a fit of gaiety, like that which comes over a man who suddenly has some great doubt or scruple resolved, he swore to Horatio, that he would take the ghost's word for a thousand pounds. But before he could make up his resolution as to what measures of revenge he should take, now he was certainly informed that his uncle was his father's murderer, he was

国王惊慌失措

sent for by the queen his mother, to a private conference in her closet.

It was by desire of the king that the queen sent for Hamlet, that she might signify to her son how much his late behaviour had displeased them both, and the king, wishing to know all that passed at that conference, and thinking that the too partial report of a mother might let slip some part of Hamlet's words, which it might much import the king to know, Polonius, the old counsellor of state, was ordered to plant himself behind the hangings in the queen's closet, where he might unseen hear all that passed. This artifice was particularly adapted to the disposition of Polonius, who was a man grown old in crooked maxims and policies of state, and delighted to get at the knowledge of matters in an indirect and cunning way.

Hamlet being come to his mother, she began to tax him in the roundest way with his actions and behaviour, and she told him that he had given great offence to his father, meaning the king, his uncle, whom, because he had married her, she called Hamlet's father. Hamlet, sorely indignant that she should give so dear and honoured a name as father seemed to him, to a wretch who was indeed no better than the murderer of his true father, with some sharpness replied: 'Mother, you have much offended my father.' The queen said that was but an idle answer. 'As good as the question deserved,' said Hamlet. The queen asked him if he had forgotten who it was he was speaking to? 'Alas!' replied Hamlet, 'I wish I could forget. You are the queen, your husband's brother's wife; and you are my mother: I wish you were not what you are.' 'Nay, then,' said the queen, 'if you show me so little respect, I will set those to you that can speak,' and was going to send the king or Polonius to him. But Hamlet would not let her go, now he had her alone, till he had tried if his words could not bring her to some sense of her wicked life; and, taking her by the wrist, he held her fast, and made her sit down. She, affrighted at his earnest manner, and fearful lest in his lunacy he should do her a mischief, cried out; and a voice was heard from behind the hangings: 'Help, help, the queen!' which Hamlet hearing, and verily thinking that it was the king himself there concealed, he drew his sword and stabbed at the place where the voice came from, as he would have stabbed a rat that ran there, till the voice ceasing, he concluded the person to be dead. But when he dragged for the body, it was not the king, but Polonius, the old officious counsellor, that had planted himself as a spy behind the hangings. ‘Oh me!’ exclaimed the queen, ‘what a rash and bloody deed have you done!’ ‘A bloody deed, mother,’ replied Hamlet, ‘but not so bad as yours, who killed a king, and married his brother.’ Hamlet had gone too far to leave off here. He was now in the humour to speak plainly to his mother, and he pursued it. And though the faults of parents are to be tenderly treated by their children, yet in the case of great crimes the son may have leave to speak even to his own mother with some harshness, so as that harshness is meant for her good, and to turn her from her wicked ways, and not done for the purpose of upbraiding. And now this virtuous prince did in moving terms represent to the queen the heinousness of her offence, in being so forgetful of the dead king, his father, as in so short a space of time to marry with his brother and reputed murderer: such an act as, after the vows which she had sworn to her first husband was enough to make all vows of women suspected, and ail virtue to be accounted hypocrisy, wedding contracts to be less than gamesters’ oaths, and religion to be a mockery and a mere form of words. He said she had done such a deed, that the heavens blushed at it, and the earth was sick of her because of it. And he showed her two pictures, the one of the late king, her first husband, and the other of the present king, her second husband, and he bade her mark the difference; what a grace was on the brow of his father, how like a god he looked! the curls of Apollo, the forehead of Jupiter, the eye of Mars, and a posture like to Mercury newly alighted on some heaven-kissing hill! this man, he said, had been her husband. And then he showed her whom she had got in his stead: how like a blight or a mildew he looked, for so he had blasted his wholesome brother. And the queen was sore ashamed that he should so turn her eyes inward upon her soul, which she now saw so black and deformed. And he asked her how she could continue to live with this man, and be a wife to him, who had murdered her first husband, and got the crown by as false means as a thief—and just as he spoke, the ghost of his father, such as he was in his lifetime, and such as he had lately seen it, entered the room, and Hamlet, in great terror, asked what it would have; and the ghost said that it came to remind him of the revenge he had promised, which Hamlet seemed to have forgot; and the ghost bade him speak to his mother, for the grief and terror she was in would else kill her. It then vanished, and was seen by none but Hamlet, neither could he by pointing to where it stood, or by any description, make his mother perceive it; who was terribly frightened all this while to hear him conversing, as it seemed to her, with nothing; and she imputed it to the disorder of his mind. But Hamlet begged her not to flatter her wicked soul in such a manner as to think that it was his madness, and not her own offences, which had brought his father's spirit again on the earth. And he bade her feel his pulse, how temperately it beat, not like a mad-

王后羞愧万分

man's. And he begged of her with tears, to confess herself to heaven for what was past, and for the future to avoid the company of the king, and be no more as a wife to him: and when she should show herself a mother to him, by respecting his father's memory, he would ask a blessing of her as a son. And she promising to observe his directions, the conference ended.

And now Hamlet was at leisure to consider who it was that in his unfortunate rashness he had killed: and when he came to see that it was Polonius, the father of the lady Ophelia, whom he so dearly loved, he drew apart the dead body, and, his spirits being now a little quieter, he wept for what he had done.

The unfortunate death of Polonius gave the king a presence for sending Hamlet out of the kingdom. He would willingly have put him to death, fearing him as dangerous; but he dreaded the people, who loved Hamlet, and the queen who, with all her faults, doted upon the prince, her son. So this subtle king, under presence of providing for Hamlet's safety, that he might not be called to account for Polonius' death, caused him to be conveyed on board a ship bound for England, under the care of two courtiers, by whom he despatched letters to the English court, which in that time was in subjection and paid tribute to Denmark, requiring for special reasons there pretended, that Hamlet should be put to death as soon as he landed on English ground. Hamlet, suspecting some treachery, in the night-time secretly got at the letters, and skilfully erasing his own name, he in the stead of it put in the names of those two courtiers, who had the charge of him, to be put to death: then sealing up the letters, he put them into their place again. Soon after the ship was attacked by pirates, and a sea-fight commenced; in the course of which Hamlet, desirous to show his velour, with sword in hand singly boarded the enemy's vessel; while his own ship, in a cowardly manner, bore away, and leaving him to his fate, the two courtiers made the best of their way to England, charged with those letters the sense of which Hamlet had altered to their own deserved destruction.

The pirates, who had the prince in their power, showed themselves gentle enemies; and knowing whom they had got prisoner, in the hope that the prince might do them a good turn at court in recompense for any favour they might show him, they set Hamlet on shore at the nearest port in Denmark. From that place Hamlet wrote to the king, acquainting him with the strange chance which had brought him back to his own country, and saying that on the next day he should present himself before his majesty. When he got home, a sad spectacle offered itself the first thing to his eyes.

This was the funeral of the young and beautiful Ophelia, his once dear mistress. The wits of this young lady had begun to turn ever since her poor father's death. That he should die a violent death, and by the hands of the prince whom she loved, so affected this tender young maid, that in a little time she grew perfectly distracted, and would go about giving flowers away to the ladies of the court, and saying that they were for her father's burial, singing songs about love and about death, and sometimes such as had no meaning at all, as if she had no memory of what happened to her. There was a willow which grew slanting over a brook, and reflected its leaves on the stream. To this brook she came one day when she was unwatched, with garlands she had been making, mixed up of daisies and nettles, flowers and weeds together, and clambering up to hang her garland upon the boughs of the willow, a bough broke, and precipitated this fair young maid, garland, and all that she had gathered, into the water, where her clothes bore her up for a while, during which she chanted scraps of old tunes, like one insensible to her own distress, or as if she were a creature natural to that element: but long it was not before her garments, heavy with the wet, pulled her in from her melodious singing to a muddy and miserable death. It was the funeral of this fair maid which her brother Laertes was celebrating, the king and queen and whole court being present, when Hamlet arrived. He knew not what all this show imported, but stood on one side, not inclining to interrupt the ceremony. He saw the flowers strewed upon her grave, as the custom was in maiden burials, which the queen herself threw in; and as she threw them she said: 'Sweets to the sweet! I thought to have decked thy bride-bed, sweet maid, not to have strewed thy grave. Thou shouldst have been my Hamlet's wife.' And he heard her brother wish that violets might spring from her grave: and he saw him leap into the grave all frantic with grief, and bid the attendants pile mountains of earth upon him, that he might be buried with her. And Hamlet's love for this fair maid came back to him, and he could not bear that a brother should show so much transport of grief, for he thought that he loved Ophelia better than forty thousand brothers. Then discovering himself, he leaped into the grave where Laertes was, all as frantic or more frantic than he, and Laertes knowing him to be Hamlet, who had been the cause of his father's and his sister's death, grappled him by the throat as an enemy, till the attendants parted them: and Hamlet, after the funeral, excused his hasty act in throwing himself into the grave as if to brave Laertes; but he said he could not bear that any one should seem to outgo him in grief for the death of the fair Ophelia. And for the time these two noble youths seemed reconciled.

But out of the grief and anger of Laertes for the death of his father and Ophelia, the king, Hamlet's wicked uncle, contrived destruction for Hamlet. He set on Laertes, under cover of peace and reconciliation, to challenge Hamlet to a friendly trial of skill at fencing, which Hamlet accepting, a day was appointed to

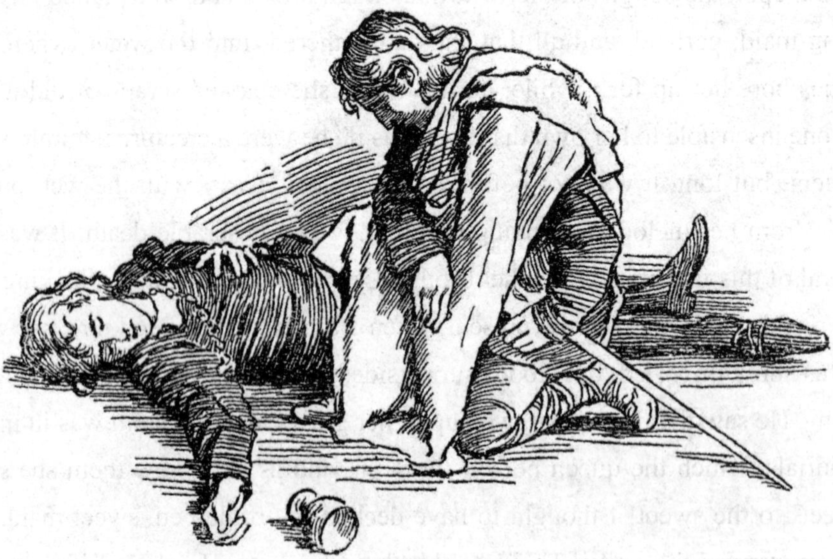

年轻人被刺伤了

try the match. At this match all the court was present, and Laertes, by direction of the king, prepared a poisoned weapon. Upon this match great wagers were laid by the courtiers, as both Hamlet and Laertes were known to excel at this sword play; and Hamlet taking up the foils chose one, not at all suspecting the treachery of Laertes, or being careful to examine Laertes' weapon, who, instead of a foil or blunted sword, which the laws of fencing require, made use of one with a point, and poisoned. At first Laertes did but play with Hamlet, and suffered him to gain some advantages, which the dissembling king magnified and extolled beyond measure, drinking to Hamlet's success, and wagering rich bets upon the issue: but after a few passes, Laertes growing warm made a deadly thrust at Hamlet with his poisoned weapon, and gave him a mortal blow. Hamlet incensed, but not knowing the whole of the treachery, in the scuffle exchanged his own innocent weapon for Laertes' deadly one, and with a thrust of Laertes' own sword repaid Laertes home, who was thus justly caught in his own treachery. In this instant the queen shrieked out that she was poisoned. She had inadvertently drunk out of a bowl which the king had prepared for Hamlet, in case, that being warm in fencing, he should call for drink: into this the treacherous king had infused a deadly poison, to make sure of Hamlet, if Laertes had failed. He had forgotten to warn the queen of the bowl, which she drank of, and immediately died, exclaiming with her last breath that she was poisoned. Hamlet, suspecting some treachery, ordered the doors to be shut, while he sought it out. Laertes told him to seek no farther for he was the traitor, and feeling his life go away with the wound which Hamlet had given him, he made confession of the treachery he had used, and now he had fallen a victim to it: and he told Hamlet of the envenomed point, and said that Hamlet had not half an hour to live, for no medicine could cure him; and begging forgiveness of Hamlet, he died, with his last words accusing the king of being the contriver of the mischief. When Hamlet saw his end draw near, there being yet some venom left upon the sword, he suddenly turned upon his false uncle, and thrust the point of it to his heart, fulfilling the promise which he had made to his father's spirit, whose injunction was now accomplished, and his foul murder revenged upon the murderer. Then Hamlet, feeling his breath fail and life departing, turned to his dear friend Horatio, who had been spectator of this fatal tragedy; and with his dying breath requested him that he would live to tell his story to the world (for Horatio had made a motion as if he would slay himself to accompany the prince in death), and Horatio promised that he would make a true report, as one that was privy to all the circumstances. And, thus satisfied, the noble heart of Hamlet cracked; and Horatio and the bystanders with many tears commended the spirit of this sweet prince to the guardianship of angels. For Hamlet was a loving and a gentle prince, and greatly beloved for his many noble and princelike qualities; and if he had lived, would no doubt have proved a most royal and complete king to Denmark.

老国王终于安息了

奥赛罗

Othello

导 读

黛丝狄蒙娜不仅拥有美貌，同时也拥有父亲留给她的巨额财富，所以有好多人追求她。但是她喜欢上了一个摩尔人——奥赛罗。

奥赛罗除了皮肤是黑的，其他都值得称道。他是一名百战百胜的将军，还曾经是一个旅行家。他见多识广，又很健谈，深深吸引了黛丝狄蒙娜。黛丝狄蒙娜巧妙地向奥赛罗表达了爱意，于是奥赛罗向她求婚了。但是黛丝狄蒙娜的父亲勃拉班提奥并不同意这门婚事。他去控诉奥赛罗欺骗自己的女儿。

偏巧这时土耳其人来进攻威尼斯，元老们认为只有奥赛罗才能够打败土耳其人。在审判过程中，奥赛罗向元老们讲述了自己同黛丝狄蒙娜的爱情，黛丝狄蒙娜亲自到元老院做证。最后，勃拉班提奥不得不承认奥赛罗是自己的女婿，他也同意把女儿嫁给他。随后，奥赛罗带着妻子出征了。还没等到达战场，就听说土耳其的舰队被暴风吹散了。可是一场更大的危机悄悄来临了。

奥赛罗的朋友凯西欧是一个讨女人喜欢的小伙子，当初奥赛罗追求黛丝狄蒙娜的时候，凯西欧就帮过忙。将军结婚之后，凯西欧还常常去将军家做客。最近，奥赛罗提升凯西欧做了副官，这让一名叫做依阿古的军官十分嫉妒。他想出了一条恶毒的计策，要让奥赛罗、黛丝狄蒙娜、凯西欧一起毁灭。

一天夜里，凯西欧负责夜间巡逻，依阿古找到机会不停地劝他喝酒，还派人找碴儿和凯西欧决斗，最终形成了骚乱，把奥赛罗都惊醒了。最后，奥赛罗只好解除了凯西欧副官的职务。

凯西欧十分懊悔。这时依阿古劝凯西欧去找黛丝狄蒙娜说说，让她出面向将军求情，将军一定会答应的。于是凯西欧就去找了黛丝狄蒙娜。在他和黛丝狄蒙娜说话的时候，依阿古引着奥德赛从房门经过，还说了好多添油加醋的话。这让奥赛罗起了疑心。

后来，依阿古几次三番的挑拨，逐渐地，奥赛罗开始怀疑自己的妻子真的和凯西欧有着不道德的关系了。最终他决定派依阿古去杀死凯西欧。而他自己在极不理智的情况下决定杀死自己的妻子。

美丽的黛丝狄蒙娜被奥赛罗刺死了，这时伤重的凯西欧出现在奥赛罗的家，他杀死了依阿古派去的刺客，找到了依阿古陷害他们的证据。奥赛罗深深地自责，在妻子的面前自杀了。奥赛罗的继任者听说了依阿古的罪行，就用最严厉的刑罚惩治了这个恶棍。

人物事件词汇表

Venice	威尼斯 意大利东北部城市，亚得里亚海威尼斯湾西北岸重要港口
Moor	摩尔 非洲西北部的一个民族
Desdemona	黛丝狄蒙娜 威尼斯的美女
Brabantio	勃拉班提奥 威尼斯元老，黛丝狄蒙娜的父亲
Othello	奥赛罗 威尼斯将军，故事的主人公
Cassio	凯西欧 奥赛罗的朋友
Iago	依阿古 奥赛罗手下资格较老的军官，为人奸诈险恶

Brabantio, the rich senator of Venice, had a fair daughter, the gentle Desdemona. She was sought to by divers suitors, both on account of her many virtuous qualities, and for her rich expectations. But among the suitors of her own clime and complexion, she saw none whom she could affect: for this noble lady, who regarded the mind more than the features of men, with a singularity rather to be admired than imitated, had chosen for the object of her affections, a Moor, a black, whom her father loved, and often invited to his house.

Neither is Desdemona to be altogether condemned for the unsuitableness of the person whom she selected for her lover. Bating that Othello was black, the noble Moor wanted nothing which might recommend him to the affections of the greatest lady. He was a soldier, and a brave one; and by his conduct in bloody wars against the Turks, had risen to the rank of general in the Venetian service, and was esteemed and trusted by the state.

He had been a traveller, and Desdemona (as is the manner of ladies) loved to hear him tell the story of his adventures, which he would run through from his earliest recollection; the battles, sieges, and encounters, which he had passed through; the perils he had been exposed to by land and by water; his hair-breadth escapes, when he had entered a breach, or marched up to the mouth of a cannon; and how he had been taken prisoner by the insolent enemy, and sold to slavery; how he demeaned himself in that state, and how he escaped: all these accounts, added to the narration of the strange things he had seen in foreign countries, the vast wilderness and romantic caverns, the quarries, the rocks and mountains, whose heads are in the clouds; of the savage nations, the cannibals who are man-eaters, and a race of people in Africa whose heads do grow beneath their shoulders: these travellers' stories would so enchain the attention of Desdemona, that if she were called off at any time by household affairs, she would despatch with all haste that business, and return, and with a greedy ear devour Othello's discourse. And once he took advantage of a pliant hour, and drew from her a prayer, that he would tell her the whole story of his life at large, of which she had heard so much, but only by parts: to which he consented, and beguiled her of many a tear, when he spoke of some distressful stroke which his youth had suffered.

His story being done, she gave him for his pains a world of sighs: she swore a pretty oath, that it was all passing strange, and pitiful, wondrous pitiful: she wished (she said) she had not heard it, yet she wished that heaven had made her such a man; and then she thanked him, and told him, if he had a friend who loved her, he had only to teach him how to tell his story, and that would woo her. Upon this hint, delivered not with more frankness than modesty, accompanied with certain bewitching prettiness, and blushes, which Othello could not but understand, he spoke more openly of his love, and in this golden opportunity gained the consent of the generous lady Desdemona privately to marry him.

Neither Othello's colour nor his fortune were such that it could be hoped Brabantio would accept him for a con-in-law. He had left his daughter free; but he did expect that, as the manner of noble Venetian ladies was, she would choose ere long a husband of senatorial rank or expectations; but in this he was deceived; Desdemona loved the Moor, though he was black, and devoted her heart and fortunes to his valiant parts and qualities; so was her heart subdued to an implicit devotion to the man she had selected for a husband, that his very colour, which to all but this discerning lady would have proved an insurmountable objection, was by her esteemed above all the white skins and clear complexions of the young Venetian nobility, her suitors.

Their marriage, which, though privately carried, could not long be kept a secret, came to the ears of the old man, Brabantio, who appeared in a solemn council of the senate, as an accuser of the Moor Othello, who by spells and witchcraft (he maintained) had seduced the affections of the fair Desdemona to marry him, without the consent of her father, and against the obligations of hospitality.

At this juncture of time it happened that the state of Venice had immediate need of the services of Othello, news having arrived that the Turks with mighty preparation had fitted out a fleet, which was bending its course to the island of Cyprus, with intent to regain that strong post from the Venetians, who then held it; in this emergency the state turned its eyes upon Othello, who alone was deemed adequate to conduct the defence of Cyprus against the Turks. So that Othello, now summoned before the senate, stood in their presence at once as a candidate for a great state employment, and as a culprit, charged with offences which by the laws of Venice were made capital.

The age and senatorial character of old Brabantio, commanded a most patient hearing from that grave assembly; but the incensed father conducted his accusation with so much intemperance, producing likelihoods and allegations for proofs, that, when Othello was called upon for his defence, he had only to relate a plain tale of the course of his love; which he did with such an artless eloquence, recounting the whole story of his wooing, as we have related it above, and delivered his speech with so noble a plainness (the evidence of truth), that the duke, who sat as chief judge, could not help confessing that a tale so told would have won his daughter too: and the spells and conjurations which Othello had used in his courtship, plainly appeared to have been no more than the honest arts of men in love; and the only witchcraft which he had used, the faculty of telling a soft tale to win a lady's ear.

This statement of Othello was confirmed by the testimony of the lady Desdemona herself, who appeared in court, and professing a duty to her father for life and education, challenged leave of him to profess a yet higher duty to her lord and husband, even so much as her mother had shown in preferring him (Brabantio) above her father.

The old senator, unable to maintain his plea, called the Moor to him with many expressions of sorrow, and, as an act of necessity, bestowed upon him his daughter, whom, if he had been free to withhold her (he told him), he would with all his heart have kept from him; adding, that he was glad at soul that he had no other child, for this behaviour of Desdemona would have taught him to be a tyrant, and hang clogs on them for her desertion.

This difficulty being got over. Othello, to whom custom had rendered the hardships of a military life as natural as food and rest are to other men, readily undertook the management of the wars in Cyprus: and Desdemona, preferring the honour of her lord (though with danger) before the indulgence of those idle delights in which new-married people usually waste their time, cheerfully consented to his going.

No sooner were Othello and his lady landed in Cyprus, than news arrived, that a desperate tempest had dispersed the Turkish fleet, and thus the island was secure from any immediate apprehension of an attack. But the war, which Othello was to suffer, was now beginning; and the enemies, which malice stirred up against his innocent lady, proved in their nature more deadly than strangers or infidels.

Among all the general's friends no one possessed the confidence of Othello more entirely than Cassio. Michael Cassio was a young soldier, a Florentine, gay, amorous, and of pleasing address, favourite qualities with women; he was handsome and eloquent, and exactly such a person as might alarm the jealousy of a man advanced in years (as Othello in some measure was), who had married a young and beautiful wife; but Othello was as free from jealousy as he was noble, and as incapable of suspecting as of doing a base action. He had employed this Cassio in his love affair with Desdemona, and Cassio had been a sort of go-between in his suit: for Othello, fearing that himself had not those soft parts of conversation which please ladies, and finding these qualities in his friend, would often depute Cassio to go (as he phrased it) a courting for him: such innocent simplicity being rather an honour than a blemish to the character of the valiant Moor. So that no wonder, if next to Othello himself (but at far distance, as beseems a virtuous wife) the gentle Desdemona loved and trusted Cassio. Nor had the marriage of this couple made any difference in their behaviour to Michael Cassio. He frequented their house, and his free and rattling talk was no unpleasing variety to Othello, who was himself of a more serious temper: for such tempers are observed often to delight in their contraries, as a relief from the oppressive excess of their own: and Desdemona and Cassio would talk and laugh together, as in the days when he went a courting for his friend.

Othello had lately promoted Cassio to be the lieutenant, a place of trust, and nearest to the general's person. This promotion gave great offence to Iago, an older officer who thought he had a better claim than Cassio, and would often ridicule Cassio as a fellow fit only for the company of ladies, and one that knew no more of the art of war or how to set an army in array for battle, than a girl. Iago hated Cassio, and he hated Othello, as well for favouring Cassio, as for an unjust suspicion, which he had lightly taken up against Othello that the Moor was too fond of Iago's wife Emilia. From these imaginary provocations, the plotting mind of Iago conceived a horrid scheme of revenge, which should involve both Cassio, the Moor, and Desdemona, in one common ruin.

Iago was artful, and had studied human nature deeply, and he knew that of all the torments which afflict the mind of man (and far beyond bodily torture), the pains of jealousy were the most intolerable, and had the sorest sting. If he could succeed in making Othello jealous of Cassio, he thought it would be an exquisite plot of revenge, and might end in the death of Cassio or Othello, or both; he cared not.

The arrival of the general and his lady, in Cyprus, meeting with the news of the dispersion of the enemy's fleet, made a sort of holiday in the island. Everybody gave themselves up to feasting and making merry. Wine flowed in abundance, and cups went round to the health of the black Othello, and his lady the fair Desdemona.

Cassio had the direction of the guard that night, with a charge from Othello to keep the soldier from excess in drinking, that no brawl might arise, to fright the inhabitants, or disgust them with the new-landed forces. That night Iago began his deep-laid plans of mischief: under colour of loyalty and love to the general, he enticed Cassio to make rather too free with the bottle (a great fault in an officer upon guard). Cassio for a time resisted, but he could not long hold out against the honest freedom which Iago knew how to put on, but kept swallowing glass after glass (as Iago still plied him with drink and encouraging songs), and Cassio's tongue ran over in praise of the lady Desdemona, whom he again and again toasted, affirming that she was a most exquisite lady: until at last the enemy which he put into his mouth stole away his brains; and upon some provocation given him by a fellow whom Iago had set on, swords were drawn, and Montano, a worthy officer, who interfered to appease the dispute, was wounded in the scuffle. The riot now began to be general, and Iago, who had set on foot the mischief, was foremost in spreading the alarm, causing the castle-bell to be rung (as if some dangerous mutiny instead of a slight drunken quarrel had arisen): the alarm-bell ringing awakened Othello, who, dressing in a hurry, and coming to the scene of action, questioned Cassio of the cause. Cassio was now come to himself, the effect of the wine having a little gone off, but was too much ashamed to reply; and Iago, pretending a great reluctance to accuse Cassio, but, as it were, forced into it by Othello, who insisted to know the truth, gave an account of the whole matter (leaving out his own share in it, which Cassio was too far gone to remember) in such a manner, as while he seemed to make Cassio's offence less, did indeed make it appear greater than it was. The result was, that Othello, who was a strict observer of discipline, was compelled to take away Cassio's place of lieutenant from him.

Thus did Iago's first artifice succeed completely; he had now undermined his hated rival, and thrust him out of his place: but a further use was hereafter to be made of the adventure of this disastrous night.

Cassio, whom this misfortune had entirely sobered, now lamented to his seeming friend Iago that he should have been such a fool as to transform himself into a beast. He was undone, for how could he ask the general for his place again? he would tell him he was a drunkard. He despised himself. Iago, affecting to make light of it, said, that he, or any man living, might be drunk upon occasion; it remained now to make the best of a bad bargain; the general's wife was now the general, and could do anything with Othello; that he were best to apply to the lady Desdemona to mediate for him with her lord; that she was of a frank, obliging disposition, and would readily undertake a good office of this sort, and set Cassio right again in the general's favour; and then this crack in their love would be made stronger than ever. A good advice of Iago, if it had not been given for wicked purposes, which will after appear.

Cassio did as Iago advised him, and made application to the lady Desdemona, who was easy to be won over in any honest suit; and she promised Cassio that she should be his solicitor with her lord, and rather die than give up his cause. This she immediately set about in so earnest and pretty a manner, that Othello, who was mortally offended with Cassio, could not put her off. When he pleaded delay, and that it was too soon to pardon such an offender, she would not be beat back, but insisted that it should be the next night, or the morning after, or the next morning to that at farthest. Then she showed how penitent and humbled poor Cassio was, and that his offence did not deserve so sharp a check. And when Othello still hung back: 'What! my lord,' said she, 'that I should have so much to do to plead for Cassio, Michael Cassio, that came a courting for you, and oftentimes, when I have spoken in dispraise of you, has taken your part! I count this but a little thing to ask of you. When I mean to try your love indeed, I shall ask a weighty matter.' Othello could deny nothing to such a pleader, and only requesting that Desdemona would leave the time to him, promised to receive Michael Cassio again in favour.

It happened that Othello and Iago had entered into the room where Desdemona was, just as Cassio, who had been imploring her intercession, was departing at the opposite door: and Iago, who was full of art, said in a low voice, as if to himself: 'I like not that.' Othello took no great notice of what he said; indeed, the conference which immediately took place with his lady put it out of his head; but he remembered it afterwards. For when Desdemona was gone, Iago, as if for mere satisfaction of his thought, questioned Othello whether Michael Cassio, when Othello was courting his lady, knew of his love. To this the general answering in the affirmative, and adding, that he had gone between them very often during the courtship, Iago knitted his brow, as if he had got fresh light on some terrible matter, and cried: 'Indeed!' This brought into Othello's mind the words which Iago had let fall upon entering the room, and seeing Cassio with Desdemona; and he began to think there was some meaning in all this: for he deemed Iago to be a just man, and full of love and honesty, and what in a false knave would be tricks, in him seemed to be the natural workings of an honest mind, big with something too great for utterance: and Othello prayed Iago to speak what he knew, and to give his worst thoughts words. 'And what,' said Iago, 'if some thoughts very vile should have intruded into my breast, as where is the palace into which foul things do not enter?' Then Iago went on to say, what a pity it were, if any trouble should arise to Othello out of his imperfect observations; that it would not be for Othello's peace to know his thoughts; that people's good names were not to be taken away for slight suspicions; and when Othello's curiosity was raised almost to distraction with these hints and scattered words, Iago, as if in earnest care for Othello's peace of mind, besought him to beware of jealousy: with such art did this villain raise suspicions in the unguarded Othello, by the very caution which he pretended to give him against suspicion. 'I know,' said Othello, 'that my wife is fair, loves company and feasting, is free of speech, sings, plays, and dances well: but where virtue is, these qualities are virtuous. I must have proof before I think her dishonest.' Then Iago, as if glad that Othello was slow to believe ill of his lady, frankly declared that he had no proof, but begged Othello to observe her behaviour well, when Cassio was by; not to be jealous nor too secure neither, for that he (Iago) knew the dispositions of the Italian ladies, his countrywomen, better than Othello could do; and that in Venice the wives let heaven see many pranks they dared not show their husbands. Then he artfully insinuated that Desdemona deceived her father in marrying with Othello, and carried it so closely, that the poor old man thought that witchcraft had been used. Othello was much moved with this argument, which brought the matter home to him, for if she had deceived her father, why might she not deceive her husband?

Iago begged pardon for having moved him; but Othello, assuming an indifference, while he was really shaken with inward grief at Iago's words, begged him to go on, which Iago did with many apologies, as if unwilling to produce anything against Cassio, whom he called his friend: he then came strongly to the point, and reminded Othello how Desdemona had refused many suitable matches of her own clime and complexion, and had married him, a Moor, which showed unnatural in her, and proved her to have a headstrong will; and when her better judgment returned, how probable it was she should fall upon comparing Othello with the fine forms and clear white complexions of the young Italians her countrymen. He concluded with advising Othello to put off his reconcilement with Cassio a little longer, and in the meanwhile to note with what earnestness Desdemona should intercede in his behalf; for that much would be seen in that. So mischievously did this artful villain lay his plots to turn the gentle qualities of this innocent lady into her destruction, and make a net for her out of her own goodness to entrap her: first setting Cassio on to entreat her mediation, and then out of that very mediation contriving stratagems for her ruin.

The conference ended with Iago's begging Othello to account his wife innocent, until he had more decisive proof; and Othello promised to be patient; but from that moment the deceived Othello never tasted content of mind. Poppy, nor the juice of mandragora, nor all the sleeping potions in the world, could ever again restore to him that sweet rest, which he had enjoyed but yesterday. His occupation sickened upon him. He no longer took delight in arms. His heart, that used to be roused at the sight of troops, and banners, and battle-array, and would stir and leap at the sound of a drum, or a trumpet, or a neighing war-horse, seemed to have lost all that pride and ambition which are a soldier's virtue; and his military ardour and all his old joys forsook him. Sometimes he thought his wife honest, and at times he thought her not so; sometimes he thought Iago just, and at times he thought him not so; then he would wish that he had never known of it; he was not the worse for her loving Cassio, so long as he knew it not: torn to pieces with these distracting thoughts, he once laid hold on Iago's throat, and demanded proof of Desdemona's guilt, or threatened instant death for his having belied her. Iago, feigning indignation that his honesty should be taken for a vice, asked Othello, if he had not sometimes seen a handkerchief spotted with strawberries in his wife's hand. Othello answered, that he had given her such a one, and that it was his first gift. 'That same handkerchief,' said Iago, 'did I see Michael Cassio this day wipe his face with.' 'If it be as you say,' said Othello, 'I will not rest till a wide revenge swallow them up: and first, for a token of your fidelity, I expect that Cassio shall be put to death within three days; and for that fair devil (meaning his lady), I will withdraw and devise some swift means of death for her.'

Trifles light as air are to the jealous proofs as strong as holy writ. A handkerchief of his wife's seen in Cassio's hand, was motive enough to the deluded Othello to pass sentence of death upon them both. without once inquiring how Cassio came by it. Desdemona had never given such a present to Cassio, nor would this constant lady have wronged her lord with doing so naughty a thing as giving his presents to another man; both Cassio and Desdemona were innocent of any offence against Othello: but the wicked Iago, whose spirits never slept in contrivance of villany, had made his wife (a good, but a weak woman) steal this handkerchief from Desdemona, under presence of getting the work copied, but in reality to drop it in Cassio's way, where he might find it, and give a handle to Iago's suggestion that it was Desdemona's present.

Othello, soon after meeting his wife, pretended that he had a headache (as he might indeed with truth), and desired her to lend him her handkerchief to hold to his temples. She did so. 'Not this,' said Othello, 'but that handkerchief I gave you.' Desdemona had it not about her (for indeed it was stolen, as we have related). 'How?' said Othello, 'this is a fault indeed. That handkerchief an Egyptian woman gave to my mother; the woman was a witch and could read people's thoughts: she told my mother, while she kept it, it would make her amiable, and my father would love her; but, if she lost it, or gave it away, my father's fancy would turn, and he would loathe her as much as he had loved her. She dying gave it to me, and bade me, if I ever married, to give it to my wife. I did so; take heed of it. Make it a darling as precious as your eye.' 'It is possible?' said the frighted lady. 'Tis true,' continued Othello 'it is a magical handkerchief; a sibyl that had lived in the world two hundred years, in a fit of prophetic fury worked it; the silkworms that furnished the silk were hallowed, and it was dyed in a mummy of maidens' hearts conserved.' Desdemona, hearing the wondrous virtues of the handkerchief, was ready to die with fear, for she plainly perceived she had lost it, and with it, she feared, the affections of her husband. Then Othello started, and looked as if he were going to do some rash thing, and still he demanded the handkerchief, which when she could not produce, she tried to divert her husband from too serious thoughts, and cheerfully told him she saw all his talk about the handkerchief was only to put her off from her suit about Michael Cassio, whom she went on to praise (as Iago had foretold), till Othello in perfect distraction burst out of the room, and then Desdemona, though unwillingly, began to suspect that her lord was jealous.

What cause she could have ministered to him she knew not, and then she accused herself for accusing the noble Othello, and thought to be sure that some untoward news from Venice, or some state troubles had puddled his spirits, and made his temper not so sweet as formerly. And she said: 'Men are not gods, and we must not look for that observance from them when they are married, which they show us on the bridal day.' And she beshrewed herself for so unkindly judging of his unkindness.

Again Othello and Desdemona met, and he accused her more plainly of being unfaithful, and of loving another man, but he did not name whom: and Othello wept, and Desdemona said: 'Alas! the heavy day! why do you weep?' And Othello told her, he could have borne all sorts of evils with fortitude—poverty, and disease, and disgrace; but her infidelity had broken his heart: and he called her a weed, that looked so fair, and smelled so sweet, that the sense ached at it; and wished she had never been born. And when he had left her, this innocent lady was so stupefied with wonder at her lord's untrue suspicion of her, that a weight-like sleep came over her, and she only desired her attendant to make her bed, and to lay her wedding-sheets upon it, saying, that when people teach their babes, they do it by gentle means and easy tasks, and Othello might have chid her so; for in good faith she was but a child when she was chidden. And this was all the complaint which this gentle lady made.

Desdemona being retired to bed expecting her lord would follow her, soon fell into a slumber, the effect of her troubled spirits, when Othello entered the chamber, full of the black purpose which he had meditated of putting his lady to death. But when he saw her asleep, he thought he would not shed her blood, nor scar that white skin of hers, more white than alabaster. But he was resolved she should die; else (as he said) she would live to betray more men, as she had done him. Then he kissed her for the last time (as he said), and that kiss was so sweet, that he must needs kiss her again: and he wept, but he said they were cruel tears.

Desdemona was awakened with his kisses, and she looked upon Othello, and she saw him gnaw his under lip, and roll his eyes, and she knew he was always fatal when he looked so: and he bade her prepare for death, and to say her prayers, for he would not kill her soul. And this innocent wife, as she lay at his mercy, begged for compassion, and to know her fault, and then he named Cassio, and the handkerchief which (he said) she had given him; and as the guiltless lady was proceeding to clear herself he suddenly would hear no more, but covering her up in the bed-clothes, stifled her till she died.

In this instant of time was brought into the house Cassio, wounded and bleeding, whom Iago had set one of his creatures on to assassinate; but the fellow not succeeding in his attempt to kill Cassio (whom he wounded, but not mortally), and being himself killed by Iago to prevent discovery, in his pockets were found certain letters, which made the guilt of Iago, and the innocence of Cassio, clear beyond all doubt; and Cassio now came to beg pardon of Othello, and to ask wherein he had offended him, that he had employed Iago to murder him.

This discovery was as thunderstroke to Othello, who now plainly saw that he was no better than a murderer, and that his wife (poor innocent lady) had been ever faithful to him; the extreme anguish of which discovery making life insupportable, he fell upon his sword, and throwing himself upon the body of his dear injured lady, expired.

These rash acts raised much passion of horror and amazement in the by-standers, for Othello had borne a fair reputation, and till he was wrought upon by the arts of a villain, which his own noble nature never gave him leave to suspect, he was a loving and a doting husband. He had loved not wisely, but too well; and his manly eyes (when he learned his mistake), though not used to weep on every small occasion, dropped tears as fast as the Arabian trees their gum. And when he was dead all his former merits and his valiant acts were remembered. Nothing now remained for his successor but to put the utmost censure of the law in force against Iago, who was executed with strict tortures; and to send word to the state of Venice of the lamentable death of their renowned general.

暴 风 雨

The Tempest

导 读

从前有一个岛，岛上只住着普罗斯波罗和米兰德父女俩。

普罗斯波罗用魔法解救了很多精灵，这些精灵在头目艾丽儿的带领下听从普罗斯波罗的指挥。

艾丽儿总喜欢捉弄女巫的儿子凯烈班。凯烈班继承了母亲的劣根性。所以普罗斯波罗只能派他去做些体力活。

每逢凯烈班偷懒的时候，艾丽儿就会想出很多办法捉弄他。

普罗斯波罗用魔法阻止海上的船只靠近小岛，米兰德一直不明原因。终于，普罗斯波罗告诉了女儿真相。原来普罗斯波罗本是米兰的公爵，他酷爱读书，于是把权力交给了自己的弟弟。结果他的弟弟在他的敌人的帮助下夺去了他的公国，并且放逐了他和他的女儿米兰德。幸亏有一位好心的大臣帮助了他们，他们才能来到这个岛上。之所以告诉女儿这些，是因为这天海上的大船上就有他的弟弟和他的仇人，他准备把他们都带到岛上来。

普罗斯波罗先是让艾丽儿把那不勒斯的王子带了过来。王子醒来看到了米兰德，立刻被米兰德的美貌所吸引；米兰德看到了王子也对王子一见钟情。普罗斯波罗很乐于看到这样的结局，但是他仍然为女儿担心。于是他设计了很多办法去考验两个人的爱情。两个年轻人经受住了考验。最终普罗斯波罗同意把米兰德许配给王子。

随后，普罗斯波罗又命令艾丽儿把弟弟和那不勒斯国王带了过来。他先是狠狠地训斥了他们，指出他们当初对待普罗斯波罗是多么的不道德。

普罗斯波罗

他的弟弟和那不勒斯国王都感到十分悔恨。后来，普罗斯波罗解除了伪装，与他们相认。三个人讲了和。等看到王子和米兰德在一起，大家就更高兴了。

这之后，普罗斯波罗带着女儿和众人一起回到了大陆，他要回去重新获得自己的爵位，同时也要为女儿举办盛大的婚礼。同时，他还释放了精灵们，从此精灵们也过上了自由的生活。

人物事件词汇表

Prospero　普洛斯波罗 故事的主人公

Miranda　米兰德 普罗斯波罗的女儿

Ariel　艾丽儿 岛上的精灵头目

Caliban　凯烈班 女巫的儿子

Naples　那不勒斯 意大利南部的第一大城市，坎帕尼亚大区以及那不勒斯省的首府

There was a certain island in the sea, the only inhabitants of which were an old man, whose name was Prospero, and his daughter Miranda, a very beautiful young lady. She came to this island so young, that she had no memory of having seen any other human face than her father's.

They lived in a cave or cell, made out of a rock; it was divided into several apartments, one of which Prospero called his study; there he kept his books, which chiefly treated of magic, a study at that time much affected by all learned men: and the knowledge of this art he found very useful to him; for being thrown by a strange chance upon this island, which had been enchanted by a witch called Sycorax, who died there a short time before his arrival, Prospero, by virtue of his art, released many good spirits that Sycorax had imprisoned in the bodies of large trees, because they had refused to execute her wicked commands. These gentle spirits were ever after obedient to the will of Prospero. Of these Ariel was the chief.

The lively little sprite Ariel had nothing mischievous in his nature, except that he took rather too much pleasure in tormenting an ugly monster called Caliban, for he owed him a grudge because he was the son of his old enemy Sycorax. This Caliban, Prospero found in the woods, a strange misshapen thing, far less human in form than an ape: he took him home to his cell, and taught him to speak; and Prospero would have been very kind to him, but the bad nature which Caliban inherited from his mother Sycorax, would not let him learn anything good or useful: therefore he was employed like a slave, to fetch wood, and do the most laborious offices; and Ariel had the charge of compelling him to these services.

When Caliban was lazy and neglected his work, Ariel (who was invisible to all eyes but Prospero's) would come slily and pinch him, and sometimes tumble him down in the mire; and then Ariel, in the likeness of an ape, would make mouths at him. Then swiftly changing his shape, in the likeness of a hedgehog, he would lie tumbling in Caliban's way, who feared the hedgehog's sharp quills would prick his bare feet. With a variety of suchlike vexatious tricks Ariel would often torment him, whenever Caliban neglected the work which Prospero commanded him to do.

Having these powerful spirits obedient to his will, Prospero could by their means command the winds, and the waves of the sea. By his orders they raised a violent storm, in the midst of which, and struggling with the wild sea-waves that every moment threatened to swallow it up, he showed his daughter a fine large ship, which he told her was full of living beings like themselves. 'O my dear father,' said she, 'if by your art you have raised this dreadful storm, have pity on their sad distress. See! the vessel will be dashed to pieces. Poor souls! they will all perish. If I had power, I would sink the sea beneath the earth, rather than the good ship should be destroyed, with all the precious souls within her.'

'Be not so amazed, daughter Miranda,' said Prospero; 'there is no harm done. I have so ordered it, that no person in the ship shall receive any hurt. What I have done has been in care of you, my dear child. You are ignorant who you are, or where you came from, and you know no more of me, but that I am your father, and live in this poor cave. Can you remember a time before you came to this cell? I think you cannot for you were not then three years of age.'

'Certainly I can, sir,' replied Miranda.

'By what?' asked Prospero; 'by any other house or person? Tell me what you can remember, my child.'

Miranda said: 'It seems to me like the recollection of a dream. But had I not once four or five women who attended upon me?'

Prospero answered: 'You had, and more. How is it that this still lives in your mind? Do you remember how you came here?'

'No, sir,' said Miranda, 'I remember nothing more.'

'Twelve years ago, Miranda,' continued Prospero, 'I was duke of Milan, and you were a princess, and my only heir. I had a younger brother, whose name was Antonio, to whom I trusted everything: and as I was fond of retirement and deep study, I commonly left the management of my state affairs to your uncle, my false brother (for so indeed he proved). I, neglecting all worldly ends, buried

普罗斯波罗父女

among my books, did dedicate my whole time to the bettering of my mind. My brother Antonio being thus in possession of my power, began to think himself the duke indeed. The opportunity I gave him of making himself popular among my subjects awakened in his bad nature a proud ambition to deprive me of my dukedom: this he soon effected with the aid of the king of Naples, a powerful prince, who was my enemy.'

'Wherefore,' said Miranda, 'did they not that hour destroy us?'

'My child,' answered her father, 'they durst not, so dear was the love that my people bore me. Antonio carried us on board a ship, and when we were some leagues out at sea, he forced us into a small boat, without either tackle, sail, or mast: there he left us, as he thought, to perish. But a kind lord of my court, one Gonzalo, who loved me, had privately placed in the boat, water, provisions, apparel, and some books which I prize above my dukedom.'

'O my father,' said Miranda, 'what a trouble must I have been to you then!'

'No, my love,' said Prospero, 'you were a little cherub that did preserve me. Your innocent smiles made me bear up against my misfortunes. Our food lasted till we landed on this desert island, since when my chief delight has been in teaching you, Miranda, and well have you profited by my instructions.'

'Heaven thank you, my dear father,' said Miranda 'Now pray tell me, sir, your reason for raising this sea-storm?'

'Know then,' said her father, 'that by means of this storm, my enemies, the king of Naples, and my cruel brother, are cast ashore upon this island.'

Having so said, Prospero gently touched his daughter with his magic wand, and she fell fast asleep; for the spirit Ariel just then presented himself before his master, to give an account of the tempest, and how he had disposed of the ship's company, and though the spirits were always invisible to Miranda, Prospero did not choose she should hear him holding converse (as would seem to her) with the empty air.

'Well, my brave spirit,' said Prospero to Ariel, 'how have you performed your task?'

美丽的米兰德

Ariel gave a lively description of the storm, and of the terrors of the mariners; and how the king's son, Ferdinand, was the first who leaped into the sea; and his father thought he saw his dear son swallowed up by the waves and lost. 'But he is safe,' said Ariel, 'in a corner of the isle, sitting with his arms folded, sadly lamenting the loss of the king, his father, whom he concludes drowned. Not a hair of his head is injured, and his princely garments, though drenched in the sea-waves, look fresher than before.'

'That's my delicate Ariel,' said Prospero. 'Bring him hither: my daughter must see this young prince. Where is the king, and my brother?'

'I left them,' answered Ariel, 'searching for Ferdinand, whom they have little hopes of finding, thinking they saw him perish. Of the ship's crew not one is missing; though each one thinks himself the only one saved: and the ship, though invisible to them, is safe in the harbour.'

'Ariel,' said Prospero, 'thy charge is faithfully performed: but there is more work yet.'

'Is there more work?' said Ariel. 'Let me remind you, master, you have promised me my liberty. I pray, remember, I have done you worthy service, told you no lies, made no mistakes, served you without grudge or grumbling.'

'How now!' said Prospero. 'You do not recollect what a torment I freed you from. Have you forgot the wicked witch Sycorax, who with age and envy was almost bent double? Where was she born? Speak; tell me.'

'Sir, in Algiers,' said Ariel.

'O was she so?' said Prospero. 'I must recount what you have been, which I find you do not remember. This bad witch, Sycorax, for her witchcrafts, too terrible to enter human hearing, was banished from Algiers, and here left by the

岛山的精灵

sailors; and because you were a spirit too delicate to execute her wicked commands, she shut you up in a tree, where I found you howling. This torment, remember, I did free you from.'

'Pardon me, dear master,' said Ariel, ashamed to seem ungrateful; 'I will obey your commands.'

'Do so,' said Prospero, 'and I will set you free.' He then gave orders what further he would have him do; and away went Ariel, first to where he had left Ferdinand, and found him still sitting on the grass in the same melancholy posture.

'O my young gentleman,' said Ariel, when he saw him, 'I will soon move you. You must be brought, I find, for the Lady Miranda to have a sight of your pretty person. Come, sir, follow me.' He then began singing:

'Full fathom five thy father lies.
Of his bones are coral made;
Those are pearls that were his eyes:
Nothing of him that doth fade,
But doth suffer a sea-change
Into something rich and strange.
Sea-nymphs hourly ring his knell:
Hark! now I hear them, Ding-dong, bell.'

This strange news of his lost father soon roused the prince from the stupid fit into which he had fallen. He followed in amazement the sound of Ariel's voice, till it led him to Prospero and Miranda, who were sitting under the shade of a large tree. Now Miranda had never seen a man before, except her own father.

'Miranda,' said Prospero, 'tell me what you are looking at yonder.'

'O father,' said Miranda, in a strange surprise, 'surely that is a spirit. Lord! how it looks about! Believe me, sir, it is a beautiful creature. Is it not a spirit?'

'No, girl,' answered her father; 'it eats, and sleeps, and has senses such as we have. This young man you see was in the ship. He is somewhat altered by grief, or you might call him a handsome person. He has lost his companions, and is wandering about to find them.'

王子来到岛上

Miranda, who thought all men had grave faces and grey beards like her father, was delighted with the appearance of this beautiful young prince; and Ferdinand, seeing such a lovely lady in this desert place, and from the strange sounds he had heard, expecting nothing but wonders, thought he was upon an enchanted island, and that Miranda was the goddess of the place, and as such he began to address her.

She timidly answered, she was no goddess, but a simple maid, and was going to give him an account of herself, when Prospero interrupted her. He was well pleased to find they admired each other, for he plainly perceived they had (as we say) fallen in love at first sight: but to try Ferdinand's constancy, he resolved to throw some difficulties in their way: therefore advancing forward, he addressed the prince with a stern air, telling him, he came to the island as a spy, to take it from him who was the lord of it. 'Follow me,' said he, 'I will tie you neck and feet together. You shall drink sea-water; shell-lush, withered roots, and husks of acorns shall be your food.' 'No,' said Ferdinand, 'I will resist such entertainment, till I see a more powerful enemy,' and drew his sword; but Prospero, waving his magic wand, fixed him to the spot where he stood, so that he had no power to move.

Miranda hung upon her father, saying: 'Why are you so ungentle? Have pity, sir; I will be his surety. This is the second man I ever saw, and to me he seems a true one.'

'Silence,' said the father: 'one word more will make me chide you, girl! What! an advocate for an impostor! You think there are no more such fine men, having seen only him and Caliban. I tell you, foolish girl, most men as far excel this, as he does Caliban.' This he said to prove his daughter's constancy; and she replied: 'My affections are most humble. I have no wish to see a goodlier man.'

'Come on, young man,' said Prospero to the prince; 'you have no power to disobey me.'

'I have not indeed,' answered Ferdinand; and not knowing that it was by magic he was deprived of all power of resistance, he was astonished to find himself so strangely compelled to follow Prospero: looking back on Miranda as long as he could see her, he said, as he went after Prospero into the cave: 'My spirits are all bound up as if I were in a dream; but this man's threats, and the weakness which I feel, would seem light to me if from my prison I might once a day behold this fair maid.'

英俊的王子

Prospero kept Ferdinand not long confined within the cell: he soon brought out his prisoner, and set him a severe task to perform, taking care to let his daughter know the hard labour he had imposed on him, and then pretending to go into his study, he secretly watched them both.

Prospero had commanded Ferdinand to pile up some heavy logs of wood. Kings' sons not being much used to laborious work, Miranda soon after found her lover almost dying with fatigue. 'Alas!' said she, 'do not work so hard; my father is at his studies, he is safe for these three hours; pray rest yourself.'

'O my dear lady,' said Ferdinand, 'I dare not. I must finish my task before I take my rest.'

'If you will sit down,' said Miranda, 'I will carry your logs the while.' But this Ferdinand would by no means agree to. Instead of a help Miranda became a hindrance, for they began a long conversation, so that the business of log-carrying went on very slowly.

Prospero, who had enjoined Ferdinand this task merely as a trial of his love, was not at his books, as his daughter supposed, but was standing by them invisible, to overhear what they said.

Ferdinand inquired her name, which she told, saying it was against her father's express command she did so.

Prospero only smiled at this first instance of his daughter's disobedience, for having by his magic art caused his daughter to fall in love so suddenly, he was not angry that she showed her love by forgetting to obey his commands. And he listened well pleased to a long speech of Ferdinand's, in which he professed to love her above all the ladies he ever saw.

In answer to his praises of her beauty, which he said exceeded all the women in the world, she replied: 'I do not remember the face of any woman, nor have I seen any more men than you, my good friend, and my dear father. How features are abroad, I know not: but, believe me, sir, I would not wish any companion in the world but you, nor can my imagination form any shape but yours that I could like. But, sir, I fear I talk to you too freely, and my father's precepts I forget.'

At this Prospero smiled, and nodded his head, as much as to say: 'This goes on exactly as I could wish; my girl will be queen of Naples.'

And then Ferdinand, in another fine long speech (for young princes speak in courtly phrases), told the innocent Miranda he was heir to the crown of Naples, and that she should be his queen.

'Ah! sir,' said she, 'I am a fool to weep at what I am glad of. I will answer you in plain and holy innocence. I am your wife if you will marry me.'

Prospero prevented Ferdinand's thanks by appearing visible before them.

'Fear nothing, my child,' said he; 'I have overheard, and approve of all you have said. And, Ferdinand, if I have too severely used you, I will make you rich amends, by giving you my daughter. All your vexations were but trials of your love, and you have nobly stood the test. Then as my gift, which your true love has worthily purchased, take my daughter, and do not smile that I boast she is above all praise.' He then, telling them that he had business which required his presence, desired they would sit down and talk together till he returned; and this command Miranda seemed not at all disposed to disobey.

When Prospero left them, he called his spirit Ariel, who quickly appeared before him, eager to relate what he had done with Prospero's brother and the king of Naples. Ariel said he had left them almost out of their senses with fear, at the strange things he had caused them to see and hear. When fatigued with wandering about, and famished for want of food, he had suddenly set before them a

米兰德爱上了王子

delicious banquet, and then, just as they were going to eat, he appeared visible before them in the shape of a harpy, a voracious monster with wings, and the feast vanished away. Then, to their utter amazement, this seeming harpy spoke to them, reminding them of their cruelty in driving Prospero from his dukedom, and leaving him and his infant daughter to perish in the sea; saying, that for this cause these terrors were suffered to afflict them.

The king of Naples, and Antonio the false brother, repented the injustice they had done to Prospero; and Ariel told his master he was certain their penitence was sincere, and that he, though a spirit, could not but pity them.

'Then bring them hither, Ariel,' said Prospero: 'if you, who are but a spirit, feel for their distress, shall not I, who am a human being like themselves, have compassion on them? Bring them, quickly, my dainty Ariel.'

Ariel soon returned with the king, Antonio, and old Gonzalo in their train, who had followed him, wondering at the wild music he played in the air to draw them on to his master's presence. This Gonzalo was the same who had so kindly provided Prospero formerly with books and provisions, when his wicked brother left him, as he thought, to perish in an open boat in the sea.

Grief and terror had so stupefied their senses, that they did not know Prospero. He first discovered himself to the good old Gonzalo, calling him the preserver of his life; and then his brother and the king knew that he was the injured Prospero.

Antonio with tears, and sad words of sorrow and true repentance, implored his brother's forgiveness, and the king expressed his sincere remorse for having assisted Antonio to depose his brother: and Prospero forgave them and, upon their engaging to restore his dukedom, he said to the king of Naples: 'I have a gift in store for you too'; and opening a door, showed him his son Ferdinand playing at chess with Miranda.

Nothing could exceed the joy of the father and the son at this unexpected meeting, for they each thought the other drowned in the storm.

'O wonder!' said Miranda, 'what noble creatures these are! It must surely be a brave world that has such people in it.'

The king of Naples was almost as much astonished at the beauty and excellent graces of the young Miranda, as his son had been. 'Who is this maid?' said he; 'she seems the goddess that has parted us, and brought us thus together.' 'No, sir,' answered Ferdinand, smiling to find his father had fallen into the same mistake that he had done when he first saw Miranda, 'she is a mortal but by immortal Providence she is mine; I chose her when I could not ask you, my father, for your consent, not thinking you were alive. She is the daughter to this Prospero, who is the famous duke of Milan, of whose renown I have heard so much, but never saw him till now: of him I have received a new life: he has made himself to me a second father, giving me this dear lady.'

'Then I must be her father,' said the king; 'but oh! how oddly will it sound, that I must ask my child forgiveness.'

'No more of that,' said Prospero: 'let us not remember our troubles past, since they so happily have ended.' And then Prospero embraced his brother, and again assured him of his forgiveness; and said that a wise overruling Providence had permitted that he should be driven from his poor dukedom of Milan, that his daughter might inherit the crown of Naples, for that by their meeting in this desert island, it had happened that the king's son had loved Miranda.

These kind words which Prospero spoke, meaning to comfort his brother, so filled Antonio with shame and remorse, that he wept and was unable to speak; and the kind old Gonzalo wept to see this joyful reconciliation, and prayed for blessings on the young couple.

Prospero now told them that their ship was safe in the harbour, and the sailors all on board her, and that he and his daughter would accompany them home the next morning. 'In the meantime,' says he, 'partake of such refreshments as my poor cave affords; and for your evening's entertainment I will relate the history of my life from my first landing in this desert island.' He then called for Caliban to prepare some food, and set the cave in order; and the company were astonished at the uncouth form and savage appearance of this ugly monster, who

(Prospero said) was the only attendant he had to wait upon him.

Before Prospero left the island, he dismissed Ariel from his service, to the great joy of that lively little spirit; who, though he had been a faithful servant to his master, was always longing to enjoy his free liberty, to wander uncontrolled in the air, like a wild bird, under green trees, among pleasant fruits, and sweet-smelling flowers. 'My quaint Ariel,' said Prospero to the little sprite when he made him free, 'I shall miss you; yet you shall have your freedom.' 'Thank you, my dear master,' said Ariel; 'but give me leave to attend your ship home with prosperous gales, before you bid farewell to the assistance of your faithful spirit; and then, master, when I am free, how merrily I shall live!' Here Ariel sung this pretty song:

精灵们过上了自由的生活

Where the bee sucks there suck I;
In a cowslip's bell I lie;
There I crouch when owls do cry.
On the bat's back I do fly

After summer merrily.
Merrily, merrily shall I live now
Under the blossom that hangs on the bough.'

Prospero then buried deep in the earth his magical books and wand, for he was resolved never more to make use of the magic art. And having thus overcome his enemies, and being reconciled to his brother and the king of Naples, nothing now remained to complete his happiness, but to revisit his native land, to take possession of his dukedom, and to witness the happy nuptials of his daughter and Prince Ferdinand, which the king said should be instantly celebrated with great splendour on their return to Naples. At which place, under the safe convoy of the spirit Ariel, they, after a pleasant voyage, soon arrived.

冬天的故事

Winter's Tale

导读

西西里国王里奥提斯和王后赫麦恩妮生活非常幸福。但是国王有一件事总是不能称心如意，那就是他想见见老朋友——波力克塞尼斯。当初他们一起长大，后来都被叫回去统治各自的国家。他们经常交换礼物和信件，但是已经很多年没有见面了。

经过一再邀请，波力克塞尼斯才从波希米亚来到了西西里。

最初，里奥提斯感到很快乐，每天带着王后陪着自己的老朋友聊天。过了一阵子，波力克塞尼斯要回去了，国王和王后都诚挚地挽留他。波力克塞尼斯本来拒绝了国王的挽留，但却被温柔的王后说服了。虽然里奥提斯相信自己的朋友高贵的品格，但是仍然产生了嫉妒心。这种嫉妒一发不可收拾，他命令一个大臣去毒死波力克塞尼斯。这个大臣叫做卡米罗。他知道里奥提斯的嫉妒毫无道理。于是他把国王的计划透露给波力克塞尼斯，然后和他一起逃回了波希米亚。之后就成了波力克塞尼斯的知己和宠臣。

波力克塞尼斯一逃走，嫉妒的里奥提斯更加生气了。他把王后投入到监牢里去。之后他派人去阿波罗神庙去问问神谕，他的妻子是否对自己忠诚。

波力克塞尼斯来到了西西里

王后赫麦恩妮在监牢里生了一个小女孩。她的挚友宝丽娜希望王后能够把女孩交给她，她会把女孩带给国王看，说不定国王会回心转意。但是宝丽娜的计划失败了。国王甚至把孩子丢到了荒凉的海岸。

国王要求公开审判王后，这时神谕被带了回来。神谕显示王后是清白的，一切都是国王的过错，如果国王不肯悔改，那么他将失去继承人。国王不肯相信。他要求继续审判王后，这时有人告诉国王，他的儿子死了。国王和王后都感到心痛。国王开始可怜起王后。他命令侍女把王后带走。不久，王后的朋友宝丽娜来告诉国王，王后也死了。

国王这时才相信王后是清白的。他如今情愿牺牲掉自己的王国，也要找回他丢掉的女儿。

小公主被起名叫作潘迪塔。她被好心的牧羊人收留了。渐渐地，潘迪塔长大了，越来越漂亮。

波力克塞尼斯有一个独生子弗洛里泽尔。这个年轻的王子在牧羊人家看到了美丽的潘迪塔，他一下子就爱上了这个姑娘。于是他化妆出现在牧羊人家中，同整个村子的人都熟识了。王子经常外出的消息让国王波力克塞尼斯十分担心。他也化妆去看看儿子究竟去做什么。他发现儿子在和牧羊人的女儿热恋，而且还打算和她结婚。波力克塞尼斯十分生气，他狠狠地骂了王子，坚决不允许他们在一起。

卡米罗看出王子是真心喜欢潘迪塔。于是他建议王子带着潘迪塔逃到西西里去。因为里奥提斯已经真心悔悟了，所以卡米罗可以说服他保护这对男女。

卡米罗带着这对男女逃到了西西里。里奥提斯接见了他们。他十分欢迎他们的到来，同时向王子表达了歉意，因为是自己的错才使他和波力克塞尼斯的友谊中断。同时，他看到潘迪塔，不禁想起了自己失掉的女儿。

牧羊人这时将当初捡到女孩时一起拿走的东西都拿了出来。大家这才明白，潘迪塔就是里奥提斯丢掉的女儿。

在这个欢乐的时刻，宝丽娜又巧妙地把当初假死的王后带给了国王，这让国王更加喜悦。后来波力克塞尼斯也来到了西西里，这回他不再反对儿子和潘迪塔的婚姻了。同时波力克塞尼斯和里奥提斯的友谊也回来了。

人物事件词汇表

Sicily	西西里 地中海最大和人口最稠密的岛，它属于意大利，位于亚平宁半岛的西南
Leontes	里奥提斯 西西里国王
Hermione	赫麦恩妮 西西里王后
Bohemia	波希米亚 位于现捷克共和国的中西部，历史上是一个多民族的地区，是吉普赛人的聚集地
Polixenes	波力克塞尼斯 波希米亚国王，里奥提斯的好朋友
Camilo	卡米罗 里奥提斯的正直的大臣
Paulina	宝丽娜 赫麦恩妮的挚友
Perdita	潘迪塔 里奥提斯和赫麦恩妮的女儿
Florizel	弗洛里泽尔 波力克塞尼斯的儿子

Leontes, king of Sicily, and his queen, the beautiful and virtuous Hermione, once lived in the greatest harmony together. So happy was Leontes in the love of this excellent lady, that he had no wish ungratified, except that he sometimes desired to see again, and to present to his queen, his old companion and school-fellow, Polixenes, king of Bohemia. Leontes and Polixenes were brought up together from their infancy, but being, by the death of their fathers, called to reign over their respective kingdoms, they had not met for many years, though they frequently interchanged gifts, letters, and loving embassies.

At length, after repeated invitations, Polixenes came from Bohemia to the Sicilian court, to make his friend Leontes a visit.

At first this visit gave nothing but pleasure to Leontes. He recommended the friend of his youth to the queen's particular attention, and seemed in the presence of his dear friend and old companion to have his felicity quite completed. They talked over old times; their schooldays and their youthful pranks were remembered, and recounted to Hermione, who always took a cheerful part in these conversations.

When, after a long stay, Polixenes was preparing to depart, Hermione, at the desire of her husband, joined her entreaties to his that Polixenes would prolong his visit.

And now began this good queen's sorrow; for Polixenes refusing to stay at the request of Leontes, was won over by Hermione's gentle and persuasive words to put off his departure for some weeks longer. Upon this, although Leontes had so long known the integrity and honourable principles of his friend Polixenes, as well as the excellent disposition of his virtuous queen, he was seized with an ungovernable jealousy. Every attention Hermione showed to Polixenes, though by her husband's particular desire, and merely to please him, increased the unfortunate king's jealousy; and from being a loving and a true friend, and the best and fondest of husbands, Leontes became suddenly a savage and inhuman monster. Sending for Camillo, one of the lords of his court, and telling him of the suspicion he entertained, he commanded him to poison Polixenes.

国王对波力克塞尼斯产生了嫉妒心

Camillo was a good man; and he, well knowing that the jealousy of Leontes had not the slightest foundation in truth, instead of poisoning Polixenes, acquainted him with the king his master's orders, and agreed to escape with him out of the Sicilian dominions; and Polixenes, with the assistance of Camillo, arrived safe in his own kingdom of Bohemia, where Camillo lived from that time in the king's court, and became the chief friend and favourite of Polixenes.

The flight of Polixenes enraged the jealous Leontes still more; he went to the queen's apartment, where the good lady was sitting with her little son Mamillius, who was just beginning to tell one of his best stories to amuse his mother, when the king entered, and taking the child away, sent Hermione to prison.

Mamillius, though but a very young child, loved his mother tenderly; and when he saw her so dishonoured, and found she was taken from him to be put into a prison, he took it deeply to heart, and drooped and pined away by slow degrees, losing his appetite and his sleep, till it was thought his grief would kill him.

The king, when he had sent his queen to prison, commanded Cleomenes and Dion, two Sicilian lords, to go to Delphos, there to inquire of the oracle at the temple of Apollo, if his queen had been unfaithful to him. When Hermione had been a short time in prison, she was brought to bed of a daughter; and the poor lady received much comfort from the sight of her pretty baby, and she said to it: 'My poor little prisoner, I am as innocent as you are.'

Hermione had a kind friend in the noble-spirited Paulina, who was the wife of Antigonus, a Sicilian lord; and when the lady Paulina heard her royal mistress was brought to bed, she went to the prison where Hermione was confined; and she said to Emilia, a lady who attended upon Hermione: 'I pray you, Emilia, tell the good queen, if her majesty dare trust me with her little babe, I will carry it to the king, its father; we do not know how he may soften at the sight of his innocent child.' 'Most worthy madam,' replied Emilia, 'I will acquaint the queen with your noble offer; she was wishing to-day that she had any friend who would venture to present the child to the king.' 'And tell her,' said Paulina, 'that I will speak boldly to Leontes in her defence.' 'May you be for ever blessed,' said Emilia, 'for your kindness to our gracious queen!' Emilia then went to Hermione, who joyfully gave up her baby to the care of Paulina, for she had feared that no one would dare venture to present the child to its father.

Paulina took the new-born infant, and forcing herself into the king's presence, notwithstanding her husband, fearing the king's anger, endeavoured to prevent her, she laid the babe at its father's feet, and Paulina made a noble speech to the king in defence of Hermione, and she reproached him severely for his inhumanity, and implored him to have mercy on his innocent wife and child. But Paulina's spirited remonstrances only aggravated Leontes' displeasure, and he ordered her husband Antigonus to take her from his presence.

When Paulina went away, she left the little baby at its father's feet, thinking when he was alone with it, he would look upon it, and have pity on its helpless innocence.

The good Paulina was mistaken: for no sooner was she gone than the merciless father ordered Antigonus, Paulina's husband, to take the child, and carry it out to sea, and leave it upon some desert shore to perish.

Antigonus, unlike the good Camillo, too well obeyed the orders of Leontes; for he immediately carried the child on ship-board, and put out to sea, intending to leave it on the first desert coast he could find.

So firmly was the king persuaded of the guilt of Hermione, that he would not wait for the return of Cleomenes and Dion, whom he had sent to consult the oracle of Apollo at Delphos; but before the queen was recovered from her lying-in, and from her grief for the loss of her precious baby, he had her brought to a public trial before all the lords and nobles of his court. And when all the great lords, the judges, and all the nobility of the land were assembled together to try Hermione, and that unhappy queen was standing as a prisoner before her subjects to receive their judgement Cleomenes and Dion entered the assembly, and presented to the king the answer of the oracle, sealed up; and Leontes commanded the seal to be broken, and the words of the oracle to be read aloud, and these were the words: 'Hermione is innocent, Polixenes blameless,—Camillo a true subject, Leontes a jealous tyrant, and the king shall live without an heir if that which is lost be not found.' The king would give no credit to the words of the oracle: he said it was a falsehood invented by the queen's friends, and he desired the judge to proceed in the trial of the queen; but while Leontes was speaking, a man entered and told him that the prince Mamillius, hearing his mother was to be tried for her life, struck with grief and shame, had suddenly died.

Hermione, upon hearing of the death of this dear affectionate child, who had lost his life in sorrowing for her misfortune, fainted; and Leontes, pierced to the heart by the news, began to feel pity for his unhappy queen, and he ordered Paulina, and the ladies who were her attendants, to take her away, and use means for her recovery. Paulina soon returned, and told the king that Hermione was dead.

When Leontes heard that the queen was dead, he repented of his cruelty to her; and now that he thought his ill-usage had broken Hermione's heart, he believed her innocent; and now he thought the words of the oracle were true, as he knew 'if that which was lost was not found,' which he concluded was his young daughter, he should be without an heir, the young prince Mamillius being dead; and he would give his kingdom now to recover his lost daughter: and Leontes gave himself up to remorse, and passed many years in mournful thoughts and repentant grief.

The ship in which Antigonus carried the infant princess out to sea was driven by a storm upon the coast of Bohemia, the very kingdom of the good

被熊咬死

king Polixenes. Here Antigonus landed, and here he left the little baby.

Antigonus never returned to Sicily to tell Leontes where he had left his daughter, for as he was going back to the ship, a bear came out of the woods, and tore him to pieces; a just punishment on him for obeying the wicked order of Leontes.

The child was dressed in rich clothes and jewels; for Hermione had made it very fine when she sent it to Leontes, and Antigonus had pinned a paper to its mantle, and the name of Perdita written thereon, and words obscurely intimating its high birth and untoward fate.

This poor deserted baby was found by a shepherd. He was a humane man, and so he carried the little Perdita home to his wife, who nursed it tenderly; but poverty tempted the shepherd to conceal the rich prize he had found: therefore he left that part of the country, that no one might know where he got his riches, and with part of Perdita's jewels he bought herds of sheep, and became a wealthy shepherd. He brought up Perdita as his own child, and she knew not she was any other than a shepherd's daughter.

The little Perdita grew up a lovely maiden; and though she had no better education than that of a shepherd's daughter, yet so did the natural graces she inherited from her royal mother shine forth in her untutored mind, that no one from her behaviour would have known she had not been brought up in her father's court.

Polixenes, the king of Bohemia, had an only son, whose name was Florizel. As this young prince was hunting near the shepherd's dwelling, he saw the old man's supposed daughter; and the beauty, modesty, and queen-like deportment of Perdita caused him instantly to fall in love with her. He soon, under the name of Doricles, and in the disguise of a private gentleman, became a constant visitor at the old shepherd's house. Florizel's frequent absences from court alarmed Polixenes; and setting people to watch his son, he discovered his love for the shepherd's fair daughter.

Polixenes then called for Camillo, the faithful Camillo, who had preserved

牧羊人收留了小公主

his life from the fury of Leontes, and desired that he would accompany him to the house of the shepherd, the supposed father of Perdita.

Polixenes and Camillo, both in disguise, arrived at the old shepherd's dwelling while they were celebrating the feast of sheep-shearing; and though they were strangers, yet at the sheep-shearing every guest being made welcome, they were invited to walk in, and join in the general festivity.

Nothing but mirth and jollity was going forward. Tables were spread, and great preparations were making for the rustic feast. Some lads and lasses were dancing on the green before the house, while others of the young men were buying ribands, gloves, and such toys, of a pedlar at the door.

While this busy scene was going forward, Florizel and Perdita sat quietly in a retired corner, seemingly more pleased with the conversation of each other, than desirous of engaging in the sports and silly amusements of those around them.

The king was so disguised that it was impossible his son could know him: he therefore advanced near enough to hear the conversation. The simple yet clegant manner in which Perdita conversed with his son did not a little surprise Polixenes: he said to Camillo: 'This is the prettiest low-born lass I ever saw; nothing she does or says but looks like something greater than herself, too noble for this place.'

Pamillo replied: 'Indeed she is the very queen of curds and cream.'

'Pray, my good friend,' said the king to the old shepherd, 'what fair swain is that talking with your daughter?' 'They call him Doricles,' replied the shepherd. 'He says he loves my daughter; and, to speak truth, there is not a kiss to choose which loves the other best. If young Doricles can get her, she shall bring him that he little dreams of'; meaning the remainder of Perdita's jewels; which, after he had bought herds of sheep with part of them, he had carefully hoarded up for her marriage portion.

Polixenes then addressed his son. 'How now, young man!' said he: 'your heart seems full of something that takes off your mind from feasting. When I was young, I used to load my love with presents; but you have let the pedlar go, and have bought your lass no toy.'

公主长大了

The young prince, who little thought he was talking to the king his father, replied: 'Old sir, she prizes not such trifles; the gifts which Perdita expects from me are locked up in my heart.' Then turning to Perdita, he said to her: 'O hear me, Perdita, before this ancient gentleman, who it seems was once himself a lover; he shall hear what I profess.' Florizel then called upon the old stranger to be a witness to a solemn promise of marriage which he made to Perdita, saying to Polixenes: 'I pray you, mark our contract.'

'Mark your divorce, young sir,' said the king, discovering himself. Polixenes then reproached his son for daring to contract himself to this low-born maiden, calling Perdita 'shepherd's brat, sheep-hook,' and other disrespectful names; and threatening, if ever she suffered his son to see her again, he would put her, and the old shepherd her father, to a cruel death.

The king then left them in great wrath, and ordered Camillo to follow him with prince Florizel.

When the king had departed, Perdita, whose royal nature was roused by Polixenes' reproaches, said: 'Though we are all undone, I was not much afraid; and once or twice I was about to speak, and tell him plainly that the selfsame sun which shines upon his palace, hides not his face from our cottage, but looks on both alike.' Then sorrowfully she said: 'But now I am awakened from this dream, I will queen it no further. Leave me, sir; I will go milk my ewes and weep.'

The kind-hearted Camillo was charmed with the spirit and propriety of Perdita's behaviour; and perceiving that the young prince was too deeply in love to give up his mistress at the command of his royal father, he thought of a way to befriend the lovers, and at the same time to execute a favourite scheme he had in his mind.

Camillo had long known that Leontes, the king of Sicily, was become a true penitent; and though Camillo was now the favoured friend of king Polixenes, he could not help wishing once more to see his late royal master and his native home. He therefore proposed to Florizel and Perdita that they should accompany him to the Sicilian court, where he would engage Leontes should protect them, till, through his mediation, they could obtain pardon from Polixenes, and his consent to their marriage.

To this proposal they joyfully agreed; and Camillo, who conducted everything relative to their flight, allowed the old shepherd to go along with them.

The shepherd took with him the remainder of Perdita's jewels, her baby clothes, and the paper which he had found pinned to her mantle.

After a prosperous voyage, Florizel and Perdita, Camillo and the old shep-

美丽的公主

herd, arrived in safety at the court of Leontes. Leontes, who still mourned his dead Hermione and his lost child, received Camillo with great kindness, and gave a cordial welcome to prince Florizel. But Perdita, whom Florizel introduced as his princess, seemed to engross all Leontes' attention: perceiving a resemblance between her and his dead queen Hermione, his grief broke out afresh, and he said, such a lovely creature might his own daughter have been, if he had not so cruelly destroyed her. 'And then, too,' said he to Florizel, 'I lost the society and friendship of your grave father, whom I now desire more than my life once again to look upon.'

When the old shepherd heard how much notice the king had taken of

Perdita, and that he had lost a daughter, who was exposed in infancy, he fell to comparing the time when he found the little Perdita, with the manner of its exposure, the jewels and other tokens of its high birth; from all which it was impossible for him not to conclude that Perdita and the king's lost daughter were the same.

Florizel and Perdita, Camillo and the faithful Paulina, were present when the old shepherd related to the king the manner in which he had found the child, and also the circumstance of Antigonus' death, he having seen the bear seize upon him. He showed the rich mantle in which Paulina remembered Hermione had wrapped the child; and he produced a jewel which she remembered Hermione had tied about Perdita's neck, and he gave up the paper which Paulina knew to be the writing of her husband; it could not be doubted that Perdita was Leontes' own daughter: but oh! the noble struggles of Paulina, between sorrow for her husband's death, and joy that the oracle was fulfilled, in the king's heir, his long-lost daughter being found. When Leontes heard that Perdita was his

王子爱上了潘迪塔

daughter, the great sorrow that he felt that Hermione was not living to behold her child, made him that he could say nothing for a long time, but 'O thy mother, thy mother!'

Paulina interrupted this joyful yet distressful scene, with saying to Leontes, that she had a statue newly finished by that rare Italian master, Julio Romano, which was such a perfect resemblance of the queen, that would his majesty be pleased to go to her house and look upon it, he would be almost ready to think it was Hermione herself. Thither then they all went; the king anxious to see the semblance of his Hermione, and Perdita longing to behold what the mother she never saw did look like.

When Paulina drew back the curtain which concealed this famous statue, so perfectly did it resemble Hermione, that all the king's sorrow was renewed at the sight: for a long time he had no power to speak or move.

'I like your silence, my liege,' said Paulina, 'it the more shows your wonder. Is not this statue very like your queen?'

At length the king said: 'O, thus she stood, even with such majesty, when I first wooed her. But yet, Paulina, Hermione was not so aged as this statue looks.' Paulina replied: 'So much the more the carver's excellence, who has made the statue as Hermione would have looked had she been living now. But let me draw the curtain, sire, lest presently you think it moves.'

The king then said: 'Do not draw the curtain; would I were dead! See, Camillo, would you not think it breathed? Her eye seems to have motion in it.' 'I must draw the curtain, my liege,' said Paulina. 'You are so transported, you will persuade yourself the statue lives.' 'O, sweet Paulina,' said Leontes, 'make me think so twenty years together! Still methinks there is an air comes from her. What fine chisel could ever yet cut breath? Let no man mock me, for I will kiss her.' 'Good my lord, forbear!' said Paulina. 'The ruddiness upon her lip is wet; you will stain your own with oily painting. Shall I draw the curtain?' 'No, not these twenty years,' said Leontes.

雕像动了起来

Perdita, who all this time had been kneeling, and beholding in silent admiration the statue of her matchless mother, said now: 'And so long could I stay here, looking upon my dear mother.'

'Either forbear this transport,' said Paulina to Leontes, 'and let me draw the curtain; or prepare yourself for more amazement. I can make the statue move indeed; ay, and descend from off the pedestal, and take you by the hand. But then you will think, which I protest I am not, that I am assisted by some wicked powers.'

'What you can make her do,' said the astonished king, 'I am content to hear; for it is as easy to make her speak as move.'

Paulina then ordered some slow and solemn music, which she had prepared for the purpose, to strike up; and, to the amazement of all the beholders, the statue came down from off the pedestal, and threw its arms around Leontes' neck. The statue then began to speak, praying for blessings on her husband, and on her child, the newly-found Perdita.

No wonder that the statue hung upon Leontes' neck, and blessed her husband and her child. No wonder; for the statue was indeed Hermione herself, the real, the living queen.

Paulina had falsely reported to the king the death of Hermione, thinking that the only means to preserve her royal mistress's life; and with the good Paulina, Hermione had lived ever since, never choosing Leontes should know she was living, till she heard Perdita was found; for though she had long forgiven the injuries which Leontes had done to herself, she could not pardon his cruelty to his infant daughter.

His dead queen thus restored to life, his lost daughter found, the long-sorrowing Leontes could scarcely support the excess of his own happiness.

Nothing but congratulations and affectionate speeches were heard on all sides. Now the delighted parents thanked prince Florizel for loving their lowly-seeming daughter; and now they blessed the good old shepherd for preserving their child. Greatly did Camillo and Paulina rejoice that they had lived to see so good an end of all their faithful services.

And as if nothing should be wanting to complete this strange and unlooked-for joy, king Polixenes himself now entered the palace.

When Polixenes first missed his son and Camillo, knowing that Camillo had long wished to return to Sicily, he conjectured he should find the fugitives here; and, following them with all speed, he happened to just arrive at this, the happiest moment of Leontes' life.

Polixenes took a part in the general joy; he forgave his friend Leontes the unjust jealousy he had conceived against him, and they once more loved each other with all the warmth of their first boyish friendship. And there was no fear that Polixenes would now oppose his son's marriage with Perdita. She was no 'sheep-hook' now, but the heiress of the crown of Sicily.

Thus have we seen the patient virtues of the long-suffering Hermione rewarded. That excellent lady lived many years with her Leontes and her Perdita, the happiest of mothers and of queens.

辛 白 林

Cymbeline

导 读

辛白林有三个孩子，女儿依摩琴是在王宫抚养大的，另两个孩子小时候被人偷走了。第一个妻子死后，他又结了婚。后母对待依摩琴十分残忍。她虽然憎恨依摩琴，但是又希望依摩琴能够嫁给自己和前夫的儿子，这样他的儿子就能够当不列颠的国王了。但是依摩琴没得到父亲的同意就结了婚。

波塞莫斯就是依摩琴的丈夫，是首屈一指的学者。他是辛白林收留的孩子，和依摩琴一起长大，两个人偷偷结了婚。王后把这个消息告诉了辛白林，于是辛白林流放了波塞莫斯。

波塞莫斯到了罗马城。在那里他时刻不忘自己忠贞美丽的妻子依摩琴。有一个罗马人阿埃奇摩提议和波塞莫斯打赌。他去不列颠，如果能够得到依摩琴的爱情，并且拿到当初波塞莫斯送给依摩琴的信物，那么波塞莫斯就要输给他一笔财富。波塞莫斯相信妻子的忠贞，就答应了。

阿埃奇摩向依摩琴表达爱意，被依摩琴直接拒绝了。于是阿埃奇摩卑鄙地潜入依摩琴的卧室，偷走了信物。回到罗马他拿出了信物，同时谎称得到了依摩琴的爱。这让波塞莫斯十分伤心。

波塞莫斯托朋友把依摩琴带到一个地方杀掉。可是朋友觉得波塞莫斯一定是误会了依摩琴，于是他把波塞莫斯的计划告诉了依摩琴。这让依摩琴很伤心，她决定假扮男装，去看看丈夫究竟怎么了。临走，波塞莫斯的朋友给了依摩琴一瓶药，这瓶药喝下去会让人昏睡几个小时。

依摩琴在野外遇到了波利多和凯德沃尔，两个小伙子并不知道自己是不列颠的王子，依摩琴也不知道他们就是自己的弟弟。他们共同生活了几

不列颠国王辛白林

天。后来依摩琴喝了药水，两个小伙子误以为她死了，就把她用鲜花安葬了。药力过了之后，依摩琴醒了过来，她仍然决定到罗马去。

这时候，罗马正在和不列颠作战。波塞莫斯参加了罗马的军队，他想要战死在战场上，结果他被俘虏了。

后来依摩琴和父亲相认了，同时两个小伙子也和父亲相认了。阿埃奇摩的奸计也被揭穿了。善良的人终于得到了好报。

人物事件词汇表

Cymbeline	辛白林 英国国王
Imogen	依摩琴 辛白林的女儿
Posthumus	波塞莫斯 依摩琴的丈夫
Iachimo	阿埃奇摩 罗马绅士
Polydore	波利多 辛白林的儿子
Cadwal	凯德沃尔 辛白林的儿子

During the time of Augustus Caesar, emperor of Rome, there reigned in England (which was then called Britain) a king whose name was Cymbeline.

Cymbeline's first wife died when his three children (two sons and a daughter) were very young. Imogen, the eldest of these children, was brought up in her father's court; but by a strange chance the two sons of Cymbeline were stolen out of their nursery, when the eldest was but three years of age, and the youngest quite an infant; and Cymbeline could never discover what was become of them, or by whom they were conveyed away.

Cymbeline was twice married: his second wife was a wicked, plotting woman, and a cruel stepmother to Imogen, Cymbeline's daughter by his first wife.

The queen, though she hated Imogen, yet wished her to marry a son of her own by a former husband (she also having been twice married): for by this means she hoped upon the death of Cymbeline to place the crown of Britain upon the head of her son Cloten; for she knew that, if the king's sons were not found, the princess Imogen must be the king's heir. But this design was prevented by Imogen herself, who married without the consent or even knowledge of her father or the queen.

Posthumus (for that was the name of Imogen's husband) was the best scholar and most accomplished gentleman of that age. His father died fighting in the wars for Cymbeline, and soon after his birth his mother died also for grief at the loss of her husband.

Cymbeline, pitying the helpless state of this orphan, took Posthumus (Cymbeline having given him that name, because he was born after his father's death), and educated him in his own court.

Imogen and Posthumus were both taught by the same masters, and were playfellows from their infancy; they loved each other tenderly when they were children, and their affection continuing to increase with their years, when they grew up they privately married.

The disappointed queen soon learnt this secret, for she kept spies constantly in watch upon the actions of her daughter-in-law, and she immediately told the king of the marriage of Imogen with Posthumus.

Nothing could exceed the wrath of Cymbeline, when he heard that his daughter had been so forgetful of her high dignity as to marry a subject. He commanded Posthumus to leave Britain, and banished him from his native country for ever.

The queen, who pretended to pity Imogen for the grief she suffered at losing her husband, offered to procure them a private meeting before Posthumus set out on his journey to Rome, which place he had chosen for his residence in his banishment: this seeming kindness she showed, the better to succeed in her

依摩琴和波塞莫斯

future designs in regard to her son Cloten; for she meant to persuade Imogen, when her husband was gone, that her marriage was not lawful, being contracted without the consent of the king.

Imogen and Posthumus took a most affectionate leave of each other. Imogen gave her husband a diamond ring, which had been her mother's, and Posthumus promised never to part with the ring; and he fastened a bracelet on the arm of his wife, which he begged she would preserve with great care, as a token of his love; they then bid each other farewell, with many vows of everlasting love and fidelity.

Imogen remained a solitary and dejected lady in her father's court, and Posthumus arrived at Rome, the place he had chosen for his banishment.

Posthumus fell into company at Rome with some gay young men of different nations, who were talking freely of ladies: each one praising the ladies of his own country, and his own mistress. Posthumus, who had ever his own dear lady in his mind, affirmed that his wife, the fair Imogen, was the most virtuous, wise, and constant lady in the world.

One of those gentlemen, whose name was Iachimo, being offended that a lady of Britain should be so praised above the Roman ladies, his country-women, provoked Posthumus by seeming to doubt the constancy of his so highly-praised wife; and at length, after much altercation, Posthumus consented to a proposal of Iachimo's, that he (Iachimo) should go to Britain, and endeavour to gain the love of the married Imogen. They then laid a wager, that if Iachimo did not succeed in this wicked design, he was to forfeit a large sum of money; but if he could win Imogen's favour, and prevail upon her to give him the bracelet which Posthumus had so earnestly desired she would keep as a token of his love, then the wager was to terminate with Posthumus giving to Iachimo the ring, which was Imogen's love present when she parted with her husband. Such firm faith had Posthumus in the fidelity of Imogen, that he thought he ran no hazard in this trial of her honour.

Iachimo, on his arrival in Britain, gained admittance, and a courteous welcome from Imogen, as a friend of her husband; but when he began to make professions of love to her, she repulsed him with disdain, and he soon found that he could have no hope of succeeding in his dishonourable design.

The desire Iachimo had to win the wager made him now have recourse to a stratagem to impose upon Posthumus, and for this purpose he bribed some of Imogen's attendants, and was by them conveyed into her bedchamber, concealed in a large trunk, where he remained shut up till Imogen was retired to rest, and had fallen asleep; and then getting out of the trunk, he examined the chamber with great attention, and wrote down everything he saw there, and particularly noticed a mole which he observed upon Imogen's neck, and then softly unloosing the bracelet from her arm, which Posthumus had given to her, he retired into the chest again; and the next day he set off for Rome with great expedition, and boasted to Posthumus that Imogen had given him the bracelet, and likewise permitted him to pass a night in her chamber: and in this manner Iachimo told his

阿埃奇摩藏进了箱子里

false tale: 'Her bedchamber,' said he, 'was hung with tapestry of silk and silver, the story was the proud Cleopatra when she met her Anthony, a piece of work most bravely wrought.'

'This is true,' said Posthumus; 'but this you might have heard spoken of without seeing.'

'Then the chimney,' said Iachimo, 'is south of the chamber, and the chimney-piece is Diana bathing; never saw I figures livelier expressed.'

'This is a thing you might have likewise heard,' said Posthumus, 'for it is much talked of.'

Iachimo as accurately described the roof of the chamber; and added: 'I had almost forgot her andirons; they were two winking Cupids made of silver, each on one foot standing.' He then took out the bracelet, and said: 'Know you this jewel, sir? She gave me this. She took it from her arm. I see her yet; her pretty action did outsell her gift, and yet enriched it too. She gave it me, and said, she prized it once.' He last of all described the mole he had observed upon her neck.

Posthumus, who had heard the whole of this artful recital in an agony of doubt, now broke out into the most passionate exclamations against Imogen. He delivered up the diamond ring to Iachimo, which he had agreed to forfeit to him, if he obtained the bracelet from Imogen.

Posthumus then in a jealous rage wrote to Pisanio, a gentleman of Britain, who was one of Imogen's attendants, and had long been a faithful friend to Posthumus; and after telling him what proof he had of his wife's disloyalty, he desired Pisanio would take Imogen to Milford-Haven, a seaport of Wales, and there kill her. And at the same time he wrote a deceitful letter to Imogen desiring her to go with Pisanio, for that finding he could live no longer without seeing her, though he was forbidden upon pain of death to return to Britain, he would come to Milford-Haven, at which place he begged she would meet him. She, good unsuspecting lady, who loved her husband above all things, and desired more than her life to see him, hastened her departure with Pisanio, and the same night she received the letter she set out.

卑鄙的阿埃奇摩

When their journey was nearly at an end, Pisanio, who, though faithful to Posthumus, was not faithful to serve him in an evil deed, disclosed to Imogen the cruel order he had received.

Imogen, who, instead of meeting a loving and beloved husband, found herself doomed by that husband to suffer death, was afflicted beyond measure.

Pisanio persuaded her to take comfort, and wait with patient fortitude for the time when Posthumus should see and repent his injustice: in the meantime, as she refused in her distress to return to her father's court, he advised her to dress herself in boy's clothes for more security in travelling; to which device she agreed, and thought in that disguise she would go over to Rome, and see her husband, whom, though he had used her so barbarously, she could not forget to love.

When Pisanio had provided her with her new apparel, he left her to her uncertain fortune, being obliged to return to court; but before he departed he gave her a phial of cordial, which he said the queen had given him as a sovereign remedy in all disorders.

The queen, who hated Pisanio because he was a friend to Imogen and Posthumus, gave him this phial, which she supposed contained poison, she having ordered her physician to give her some poison, to try its effects (as she said) upon animals; but the physician, knowing her malicious disposition, would not trust her with real poison, but gave her a drug which would do no other mischief than causing a person to sleep with every appearance of death for a few hours.

This mixture, which Pisanio thought a choice cordial, he gave to Imogen, desiring her, if she found herself ill upon the road, to take it; and so, with blessings and prayers for her safety and happy deliverance from her undeserved troubles, he left her.

Providence strangely directed Imogen's steps to the dwelling of her two brothers, who had been stolen away in their infancy. Bellarius, who stole them away, was a lord in the court of Cymbeline, and having been falsely accused to the king of treason, and banished from the court, in revenge he stole away the two sons of Cymbeline, and brought them up in a forest, where he lived

依摩琴去找波塞莫斯

concealed in a cave. He stole them through revenge, but he soon loved them as tenderly as if they had been his own children, educated them carefully, and they grew up fine youths, their princely spirits leading them to bold and daring actions; and as they subsisted by hunting, they were active and hardy, and were always pressing their supposed father to let them seek their fortune in the wars.

At the cave where these youths dwelt it was Imogen's fortune to arrive. She had lost her way in a large forest, through which her road lay to Milford-Haven (from which she meant to embark for Rome); and being unable to find any place where she could purchase food, she was with weariness and hunger almost dying; for it is not merely putting on a man's apparel that will enable a young lady, tenderly brought up, to bear the fatigue of wandering about lonely forests like a man. Seeing this cave, she entered, hoping to find someone within of whom she could procure food. She found the cave empty, but looking about she discovered some cold meat, and her hunger was so pressing, that she could not wait for an invitation, but sat down and began to eat. 'Ah,' said she, talking to herself, 'I see a man's life is a tedious one; how tired am I! for two nights together I have made the ground my bed: my resolution helps me, or I should be sick. When Pisanio showed me Milford-Haven from the mountain top, how near it seemed!' Then the thoughts of her husband and his cruel mandate came across her, and she said: 'My dear Posthumus, thou art a false one!'

The two brothers of Imogen, who had been hunting with their reputed father, Bellarius, were by this time returned home. Bellarius had given them the names of Polydore and Cadwal, and they knew no better, but supposed that Bellarius was their father; but the real names of these princes were Guiderius and Arviragus.

Bellarius entered the cave first, and seeing Imogen, stopped them, saying: 'Come not in yet; it eats our victuals, or I should think it was a fairy.'

'What is the matter, sir?' said the young men. 'By Jupiter,' said Bellarius again, 'there is an angel in the cave, or if not, an earthly paragon.' So beautiful did Imogen look in her boy's apparel.

She, hearing the sound of voices, came forth from the cave, and addressed them in these words: 'Good masters, do not harm me; before I entered your cave, I had thought to have begged or bought what I have eaten. Indeed I have stolen nothing, nor would I, though I had found gold strewed on the floor. Here is money for my meat, which I would have left on the board when I had made my meal, and parted with prayers for the provider.' They refused her money with great earnestness. 'I see you are angry with me,' said the timid Imogen; 'but, sirs, if you kill me for my fault, know that I should have died if I had not made it.'

'Whither are you bound?' asked Bellarius, 'and what is your name?'

扮成男装的依摩琴

'Fidele is my name,' answered Imogen. 'I have a kinsman, who is bound for Italy; he embarked at Milford-Haven, to whom being going, almost spent with hunger, I am fallen into this offence.'

'Prithee, fair youth,' said old Bellarius, 'do not think us churls, nor measure our good minds by this rude place we live in. You are well encountered; it is almost night. You shall have better cheer before you depart, and thanks to stay and eat it. Boys, bid him welcome.'

The gentle youths, her brothers, then welcomed Imogen to their cave with many kind expressions, saying they would love her (or, as they said, him) as a brother; and they entered the cave, where (they having killed venison when they were hunting) Imogen delighted them with her neat housewifery, assisting them in preparing their supper; for though it is not the custom now for young women of high birth to understand cookery, it was then, and Imogen excelled in this useful art; and, as her brothers prettily expressed it, Fidele cut their roots in characters, and sauced their broth, as if Juno had been sick, and Fidele were her dieter. 'And then,' said Polydore to his brother, 'how angel-like he sings!'

They also remarked to each other, that though Fidele smiled so sweetly, yet so sad a melancholy did overcloud his lovely face, as if grief and patience had together taken possession of him.

For these her gentle qualities (or perhaps it was their near relationship, though they knew it not) Imogen (or, as the boys called her, Fidele) became the doting-piece of her brothers, and she scarcely less loved them, thinking that but for the memory of her dear Posthumus, she could live and die in the cave with these wild forest youths; and she gladly consented to stay with them, till she was enough rested from the fatigue of travelling to pursue her way to Milford-Haven.

When the venison they had taken was all eaten and they were going out to hunt for more. Fidele could not accompany them because she was unwell. Sorrow, no doubt, for her husband's cruel usage, as well as the fatigue of wandering in the forest, was the cause of her illness.

They then bid her farewell, and went to their hunt, praising all the way the

遇到了两个弟弟

noble parts and graceful demeanour of the youth Fidele.

Imogen was no sooner left alone then she recollected the cordial Pisanio had given her, and drank it off, and presently fell into a sound and deathlike sleep.

When Bellarius and her brothers returned from hunting, Polydore went first into the cave, and supposing her asleep, pulled off his heavy shoes, that he might tread softly and not awake her; so did true gentleness spring up in the minds of these princely foresters; but he soon discovered that she could not be awakened by any noise, and concluded her to be dead, and Polydore lamented over her with dear and brotherly regret, as if they had never from their infancy been parted.

Bellarius also proposed to carry her out into the forest, and there celebrate her funeral with songs and solemn dirges, as was then the custom.

Imogen's two brothers then carried her to a shady covert, and there laying her gently on the grass, they sang repose to her departed spirit, and covering her over with leaves and flowers, Polydore said: 'While summer lasts and I live here, Fidele, I will daily strew thy grave. The pale primrose, that flower most like thy face; the blue-bell, like thy clear veins; and the leaf of eglantine, which is not sweeter than was thy breath; all these will I strew over thee. Yea, and the furred moss in winter, when there are no flowers to cover thy sweet corset.'

When they had finished her funeral obsequies they departed very sorrowful.

Imogen had not been long left alone, when, the effect of the sleepy drug going off, she awaked, and easily shaking off the slight covering of leaves and flowers they had thrown over her, she arose, and imagining she had been dreaming, she said: 'I thought I was a cave-keeper, and cook to honest creatures; how came I here covered with flowers?' Not being able to find her way back to the cave, and seeing nothing of her new companions, she concluded it was certainly all a dream; and once more Imogen set out on her weary pilgrimage, hoping at last she should find her way to Milford-Haven, and thence get a passage in some ship bound for Italy; for all her thoughts were still with her husband Posthumus, whom she intended to seek in the disguise of a page.

But great events were happening at this time, of which Imogen knew nothing; for a war had suddenly broken out between the Roman emperor Augustus Caesar and Cymbeline, the king of Britain; and a Roman army had landed to invade Britain, and was advanced into the very forest over which Imogen was journeying. With this army came Posthumus.

Though Posthumus came over to Britain with the Roman army, he did not mean to fight on their side against his own countrymen, but intended to join the army of Britain, and fight in the cause of his king who had banished him.

He still believed Imogen false to him; yet the death of her he had so fondly loved, and by his own orders too (Pisanio having written him a letter to say he had obeyed his command, and that Imogen was dead), sat heavy on his heart, and therefore he returned to Britain, desiring either to be slain in battle, or to be put to death by Cymbeline for returning home from banishment.

Imogen, before she reached Milford-Haven, fell into the hands of the Roman army; and her presence and deportment recommending her, she was made a page to Lucius, the Roman general.

Cymbeline's army now advanced to meet the enemy, and when they entered this forest, Polydore and Cadwal joined the king's army. The young men were eager to engage in acts of velour, though they little thought they were going to fight for their own royal father: and old Bellarius went with them to the battle. He had long since repented of the injury he had done to Cymbeline in carrying away his sons; and having been a warrior in his youth, he gladly joined the army to fight for the king he had so injured.

And now a great battle commenced between the two armies, and the Britons would have been defeated, and Cymbeline himself killed, but for the extraordinary velour of Posthumus and Bellarius and the two sons of Cymbeline. They rescued the king, and saved his life, and so entirely turned the fortune of the day, that the Britons gained the victory.

When the battle was over, Posthumus, who had not found the death he sought for, surrendered himself up to one of the officers of Cymbeline, willing to suffer the death which was to be his punishment if he returned from banishment.

Imogen and the master she served were taken prisoners, and brought before Cymbeline, as was also her old enemy Iachimo, who was an officer in the Roman army; and when these prisoners were before the king, Posthumus was brought in to receive his sentence of death; and at this strange juncture of time, Bellarius with Polydore and Cadwal were also brought before Cymbeline, to receive the rewards due to the great services they had by their velour done for the king. Pisanio, being one of the king's attendants, was likewise present.

Therefore there were now standing in the king's presence (but with very different hopes and fears) Posthumus and Imogen, with her new master the Roman general; the faithful servant Pisanio, and the false friend Iachimo; and like wise the two lost sons of Cymbeline, with Bellarius, who had stolen them away.

The Roman general was the first who spoke; the rest stood silent before the king, though there was many a beating heart among them.

Imogen saw Posthumus, and knew him, though he was in the disguise of a peasant; but he did not know her in her male attire; and she knew Iachimo, and she saw a ring on his finger which she perceived to be her own, but she did not know him as yet to have been the author of all her troubles: and she stood before her own father a prisoner of war.

Pisanio knew Imogen, for it was he who had dressed her in the garb of a boy. 'It is my mistress,' thought he; 'since she is living, let the time run on to good or bad.' Bellarius knew her too, and softly said to Cadwal: 'Is not this boy revived from death?' 'One sand,' replied Cadwal, 'does not more resemble another than that sweet rosy lad is like the dead Fidele.' 'The same dead thing alive,' said Polydore. 'Peace, peace,' said Bellarius; 'if it were he, I am sure he would have spoken to us.' 'But we saw him dead,' again whispered Polydore. 'Be silent,' replied Bellarius.

Posthumus waited in silence to hear the welcome sentence of his own death; and he resolved not to disclose to the king that he had saved his life in the battle, lest that should move Cymbeline to pardon him.

Lucius, the Roman general, who had taken Imogen under his protection as his page, was the first (as has been before said) who spoke to the king. He was a man of high courage and noble dignity, and this was his speech to the king:

'I hear you take no ransom for your prisoners, but doom them all to death: I am a Roman, and with a Roman heart will suffer death. But there is one thing for which I would entreat.' Then bringing Imogen before the king, he said: 'This boy is a Briton born. Let him be ransomed. He is my page. Never master had a page so kind, so duteous, so diligent on all occasions, so true, so nurse-like. He hath done no Briton wrong, though he hath served a Roman. Save him, if you spare no one beside.'

Cymbeline looked earnestly on his daughter Imogen. He knew her not in that disguise; but it seemed that all-powerful Nature spake in his heart, for he said: 'I have surely seen him, his face appears familiar to me. I know not why or wherefore I say, Live, boy; but I give you your life, and ask of me what boon you will, and I will grant it you. Yea, even though it be the life of the noblest prisoner I have.'

'I humbly thank your highness,' said Imogen.

What was then called granting a boon was the same as a promise to give any one thing, whatever it might be, that the person on whom that favour was conferred chose to ask for. They all were attentive to hear what thing the page would ask for; and Lucius her master said to her: 'I do not beg my life, good lad, but I know that is what you will ask for.' 'No, no, alas!' said Imogen, 'I have other work in hand, good master; your life I cannot ask for.'

This seeming want of gratitude in the boy astonished the Roman general.

Imogen then, fixing her eye on Iachimo, demanded no other boon than this: that Iachimo should be made to confess whence he had the ring he wore on his finger.

Cymbeline granted her this boon, and threatened Iachimo with the torture if he did not confess how he came by the diamond ring on his finger.

Iachimo then made a full acknowledgment of all his villany, telling, as has been before related, the whole story of his wager with Posthumus, and how he had succeeded in imposing upon his credulity.

What Posthumus felt at hearing this proof of the innocence of his lady cannot be expressed. He instantly came forward, and confessed to Cymbeline the cruel sentence which he had enjoined Pisanio to execute upon the princess; exclaiming wildly: 'O Imogen, my queen, my life, my wife! O Imogen, Imogen, Imogen!'

Imogen could not see her beloved husband in this distress without discovering herself, to the unutterable joy of Posthumus, who was thus relieved from a weight of guilt and woe, and restored to the good graces of the dear lady he had so cruelly treated.

Cymbeline, almost as much overwhelmed as he with joy, at finding his lost daughter so strangely recovered, received her to her former place in his fatherly

波塞莫斯知道了真相

affection, and not only gave her husband Posthumus his life, but consented to acknowledge him for his son-in-law.

Bellarius chose this, time of joy and reconciliation to make his confession. He presented Polydore and Cadwal to the king, telling him they were his two lost sons, Guiderius and Arviragus.

Cymbeline forgave old Bellarius; for who could think of punishments at a season of such universal happiness? To find his daughter living, and his lost sons in the persons of his young deliverers, that he had seen so bravely fight in his defence, was unlooked-for joy indeed!

Imogen was now at leisure to perform good services for her late master, the Roman general Lucius, whose life the king her father readily granted at her request; and by the mediation of the same Lucius a peace was concluded between the Romans and the Britons, which was kept inviolate many years.

How Cymbeline's wicked queen, through despair of bringing her projects to pass, and touched with remorse of conscience, sickened and died, having first lived to see her foolish son Cloten slain in a quarrel which he had provoked, are events too tragical to interrupt this happy conclusion by more than merely touching upon. It is sufficient that all were made happy who were deserving; and even the treacherous Iachimo, in consideration of his villainy having missed its final aim, was dismissed without punishment.